CLASSIFICATION: POETRY

A CIP catalogue record for this book is available from
the British Library.

Printed and bound in Great Britain.

Cover photograph of Edinburgh by Gregory Paul.

Paper used in the production of books published by
United Press comes only from sustainable forests.

ISBN 1-84436-040-7

First published in Great Britain in 2004 by
United Press Ltd
Admail 3735
London
EC1B 1JB
Tel: 0870 240 6190
Fax: 0870 240 6191
All Rights Reserved

www.unitedpress.co.uk

National Poetry Anthology 2004

This anthology features winning entries from an annual competition which is free to enter. Winners also receive a free copy of the anthology. If you would like to enter for next year's anthology, send a loose second class stamp and three poems, (20 lines and 160 words maximum each), to United Press, Admail 3735, London, EC1B 1JB by the annual closing date of June 30th. You can also call us on 0870 240 6190 or visit our website on unitedpress.co.uk

☐ *Christine Masson (left) of Sevenoaks, Kent receives her trophy from UP director, Dawn Quinn.*

CHAMPION OF CHAMPIONS

The 2003 United Press UK Poetry Champion was Kent poet Christine Masson. Her poem *Thinking Of You* was voted best of 236 prizewinning poems. "I've been writing poetry for 15 years and had some small successes, but nothing like this," said Christine, a retired legal secretary who lives in Otford, near Sevenoaks. Her win comes courtesy of the National Poetry Anthology. "It's now the biggest free to enter annual poetry contest in the UK," said a spokesman for United Press. "Anyone can submit poems. We pick over 200 regional winners and put them into the annual book - The National Poetry Anthology." All winners get a free copy and vote for their favourite poem in the book. The author gets the UK champion trophy to keep for life. Christine also received an oil painting as part of her prize. "We are adding a £1,000 cash prize this year, to reflect the growing prestige of the competition," said the spokesman. Christine added: "I'm delighted at my success in the competition and surprised that so many prizewinning poets voted for me. I feel very honoured." To enter the NPA, send up to 3 poems (160 words and 20 lines maximum each) to United Press, Admail 3735, London EC1B 1JB or ring 0870 240 6190. Entries close on June 30th 2004 and all the regional winners and the UK champion will be announced next spring.

Foreword

Even though the latest National Poetry Anthology broke records for the number of entries yet again, we are still strongly resisting the obvious next step - to start charging an entry fee.

When we began the NPA six years ago we never envisaged that it would grow this much, this quickly. Running the NPA has become a huge task, but everyone involved has coped with it more than competently - the NPA team have surpassed all expectations. But our intention was always to buck the trend of all the other big national competitions by offering a competition which allowed totally free entry.

This is what makes the NPA so unique. It's a breath of fresh air in a medium which needs all the help it can get. There's no doubt that because of the NPA, many poets have gone into print for the first time ever.

To reflect its rapidly growing prestige we have added a £1,000 cash prize to the overall winner.

As before this winner is not chosen by us. He or she is selected in a vote by all the poets included in the book.

To discover who is the winner from this volume, see next year's NPA or ring us on 0870 240 6190.

Peter Quinn, Editor

Contents

Each poet listed in this contents of the 2004 National Poetry Anthology is a winner in his or her own right. Their poems were selected as winners for their town or area in a free-to-enter annual competition which featured many thousands of entries. The winners are grouped into various regions. If you do not find a winner from your locality this is because insufficient entries were received from that area.

Nigel Lambert, Milton Keynes, Elizabeth Savage, Wantage, Miranda Latham-Jackson, Oxford, Siobhan Dowd, West Oxford, Catherine Lofthouse, Borehamwood, Hillary Taylor, Harpenden, Liz Marzano, Andover, Freya Bryant, Southampton, Liz Hanson, Fordingbridge, Laurie Reeves, Southampton, Jan Peters, Rookley.

SOUTH WEST & CHANNEL ISLANDS - Pages 61 - 90

Kerry Thompson, Yeovil, Anthony Watts, Taunton, Simon Le Merle, Radstock, Graham Jennings, Banwell, Fiona Hiern-Cooke, Bishops Lydeard, Susan Boyle, Bath, Suzanne Henslow, Nether Stowey, Michael FitzGerald, Jersey, Lesley Steadman, Lydney, Jacqueline Dench, Gloucester, Christine Wisdom, Cheltenham, Les Merton, Redruth, John Gordon, Penzance, Veronica Ferry, Poole, Brenda Smith, Gillingham, Alice Fergie, Verwood, Paula Langdon, Wimborne, Morwenna Griffiths, East Budleigh, Jacqui Fogwill, Tavistock, Brigid Gibbs, Tiverton, Sarah Bailey, Exeter, Laura Bolt, Ivybridge, Paula Kovacs, Sandford, Janet Beardsall, Ottery St Mary, Charlie Fisher, Totnes, Sarah Buckland, Exmouth, Christine Curry, Brislington, Sarah Fernandes, Westbury-on-Trym, Margaret Holli, Warmley, Ann Taylor, Trowbridge, Susan Harwood, Chippenham, Jennifer Pickup, Westbury, Susan Hart, Colerne.

EAST ANGLIA - Pages 91 - 98

David Horan, Hardwick, Rex Collinson, Cottenham, Tony Bowland, Ely, James Woodhouse, Wymondham, Daphne Stone, Sprowston, Michelle Clingan, Hadleigh, Claire Hamilton, Lowestoft, Raymond Hume, Sudbury.

EAST MIDLANDS - Pages 99 - 114

Christy Allan, Alfreton, Malise McGuire, Sinfin, Julia Westhead, New Mills, K M Abel, Wormhill, Alan Anthony, Quarndon, Matt Green, Loughborough, Una Bentley,

Market Harborough, Bette Walklate, Leicester,
Susan Barker, Gainsborough, Stephanie Tillotson, Boston,
Hilary Cairns, Retford, Martin Spooner, Worksop, Stephan
Richeux, Edwinstowe, Chris Ridge, Silverstone, Jim
Trevorrow, Corby, Monica Norgate, Oakham.

WEST MIDLANDS - Pages 115 - 124

Penelope Hart, Hereford, Caroline Ackroyd, Shrewsbury,
Nick Lawrence, Tamworth, Amanda Parkyn, Penkridge,
Elspeth Malloch, Lichfield, Catherine Roth, Burton-upon-
Trent, Dawn Vince, Rugby, Tony Elmore, Shard End,
Nathan Hawkins, Coventry, Gina Roberts, Quinton, Kate
Diaram, Walsall, Angus McLeod, Worcester, Carey Jane
Hardy, Redditch.

NORTH WEST - Pages 125 - 148

Genevieve Harding, Northwich, Lucy Roberts, Crewe,
Jennifer Adams, Bredbury, Barbara Edmondson,
Warrington, Lesley Conquest, Chester, J Buckley, Penrith,
Tracey Turner, Barrow-in-Furness, David Craig, Carnforth,
Lucy Crispin, Kendal, Susan Richardson, Longtown, Vik
Bennett, Windermere, Lyn Punt, Blackpool, Gillian
Constable, Accrington, Joy Wheatcroft, Brierfield, Dominic
Cooper, Burnley, Andy Chadwick, Preston, Scott Mallett,
Fleetwood, Peter Rigby, Clitheroe, Eileen Hudson, Rochdale,
Phil McNally, Bolton, Len Evans, Fallowfield, David Ryder,
Middleton, Jean Lees, Irlam, June Knight-Boulton, Newton-
le-Willows, J Offord, Southport, Daniel Smith, Higher
Bebington, Catherine Waud, Formby, Patricia Fleming,
Liverpool.

NORTH EAST - Pages 149 - 166

Richard Pink, Middlesbrough, Ed Turley, Wolsingham, Cyril
Matthews, Newton Aycliffe, Catherine Burgin, Darlington,
Myra Bowen, Hexham, Owen Sutherland, Hepscott,

Sunderland, Cyril Dick, Hull, Cynthia Watson, Knaresborough, Brian Morton, Redcar, Kat Dale, York, Tony Noon, Mexborough, Mary Louise Carr, Sheffield, Keith Garrett, Wath-upon-Dearne, Jean Armitage, Liversedge, Julie-Ann Maude, Morley, Barbara Roberts, Wetherby, Andy Vowles, Leeds.

WALES - Pages 167 - 180

Matt Lightfoot, Wrexham, James McKeon, Newport, Gary Price, Powys, Philip Poole, Pembroke Dock, Sue Moules, Lampeter, Alun Bannister, Bishopston, David Coleman, Mold, Joan Conway, Holywell, Philip Davies, Conwy, Tiffany Atkinson, Aberystwyth, John Latus, Johnstown, Wyn Williams, Caernarfon, B G Metcalfe, Porthcawl, Kevin Mills, Hengoed, Marc Harris, Cardiff.

NORTHERN IRELAND - Pages 181 - 186

Joseph Hughes, Newtownards, Denis O'Sullivan, Newtownabbey, Christa Brodie, Ballymena, Tony Weir, Belfast, Lisa Warr, Lisburn, Rowena Foster, Portadown.

SCOTLAND - Pages 187 - 202

Vivien Jones, Powfoot, John McLeod, Thurso, Patricia Ace, Crieff, Catherine Orr, Barrhead, Andrew Kerr, Auldgirth, Jennifer Elliott, Balmullo, R M Membury, Culloden, Graham Brown, Darnaway, Maureen Macnaughtan, Glenrothes, Jennifer Speirs, Thornhill, Colin Dennison, Stranraer, Matthew Smith-Mearns, Aberdeen, Alan Carter, Rothesay, Anne Dunford, Newton Stewart, Steven Hepburn, Edinburgh, Marta Blackadder, Tobermory, Colin Dewar, Dumfries, Louise Laurie, Ayr, Lesley-Anne Reid, Dundee.

South
East

FIRST LOVE

When you sleep I am consumed by you
An artist inspired
A moment in time, to be an eternity

When you wake I am surrounded by you
A picture hanging
Appreciated and desired

When alone I am enveloped by you
A path with no diversion
A river to the sea

When apart I am engulfed by you
Absorbed into the darkness
Crushed by the emptiness

A whole never to be parted
Growing together
My word to you my love

Rachel Swaffield, Chelmsford, Essex

MOMENTUM

Coming to rest you are never wholly still
Lying here beside me tired and quiet
And empty hours for both to fill
Somehow always hovering in the air
Is the prospect of your imminent departure
(Even taking off your dress can seem like a preparation for
leaving)

You give me odd minutes, hours, days
With a kind of glad guilt
No words are spoke but when you rise
A stricken face begs to explain
How someone somewhere
Stands waiting in the rain

Donald Carolan, Dagenham, Essex

OVERTAKING

Traffic lights
Turn red because they blush to look
At twitchy drivers who recklessly took
Such risks to pass
Just to queue before them like a class
Of infant children in a crocodile
Fools who think it is worthwhile
Fools who think it's grand
To brush Death's hand
Just to gain a yard or so
Traffic lights know
If you touch death enough he may
In his own time and way
Let you overtake others who were due
To be in his arms long before you

John Roberts, Maldon, Essex

MUMMY-TIME

I wait impatiently for her to sleep
I sing and hush, pretend to sleep myself
Until her fidgets fade to dark round staring eyes
That slowly sink to long-lashed shadows
Smiling in the hollows of her cheeks

I wait impatiently to be me again
To watch my soap or something on TV
To read my book and munch forbidden chocolate bars
To chat to friends by telephone in peace
To have time to myself

But soon I'm back beside the cot again
To watch for flickers in those dark-lash smiles
I put my face to hers and kiss
And gently blow across that much-smelled skin
With feeling tears I whisper long love words
And wait impatiently for her to wake

Patricia Gibbs-Leake, Westcliff-on-Sea, Essex

FOG

Morning waits, wearing grey,
Outside the window.
The hedgerows lie full,
Covered in cobwebs
Like diamond necklaces.
Dew seems to accentuate secrets,
And my morning is fogged over.
I cannot see where I have been,
And I cannot see where I'm going;
Whatever lies ahead I understand,
I'm not supposed to see,
But some things come speeding,
Shining out of the fog,
Like messengers from the future.
I can see clearer than ever,
That there is nothing there
To keep me by your side
Any longer.

Anne-Marie Batey, Leigh-on-Sea, Essex

FLAT IRON

The flat iron in the hearth
Beats a path
To the memories in my mind;
Where I find you waiting;
Taking me in metamorphal slumber
Through the lumber of our lives.
"This is mine," you said
When first you placed the flat iron
Beside the copper kettle,
Glowing in the spilled light
From the tulip lamp.
"It's all I have ..."
Your voice broke as you spoke
"Of my mother's."
Now the flat iron waits
For you to take it.
Now the flat iron waits
For you,
As I do.

Anthea Holland, Clacton-on-Sea, Essex

HAIR

I slice my fingers, slashing
Swathes from the forest at the nape
Of your neck. Fur piles up on your
Bare shoulders matting with the hairs
On your back. Claws flexing as I cut.
A small girl flees screaming to the
Highest tower, far away from the snick
Snack of the scissors as sun sets on the
Golden stone walls of the castle.
In another tower, a high pitched whining princeling
Winds my fingers to fly faster over your mane.
A rumbling growl plays counterpoint to
The trim, until it is over and you
Prowl upstairs to shower away
The tang of metal.

Sarah-Jane Critchley, Tunbridge Wells, Kent

STANDING

It's like finally heaving the image into focus.
I understand who is important to my breathing,
My being, as an anybody.
I have been compressed through these soggy bar table
Years,
Certain souls have made sure of that.
I am adjusting the volume on my past,
Realising that I have to leave here.
Hurt there will be,
But hurt there is, anyway.
I have to flee
Or I will stop like a full stop
In a place where the wallpaper is peeling.

Chris Silver, Gillingham, Kent

BENEATH

Beneath the linen, polyester, the silk,
Lies a face of a different ilk,
Alabaster white, dark shining black, skin freckled by the
sun.
Faintly feigned, with scars of ageing and adventure,
Aching, for the one.

To love the naked, uncovered flesh,
To adore each lump, bump and groove.
To kiss cruel calluses and languid lines caress,
Feel no necessity, our ageing skin, improve.

Instead,

Gracefully let it fall, flop and form a new you.
Greeting age and wisdom as well as vitality and youth.

Anthea Gostt, Biggin Hill, Kent

TEETH

You could always fight your corner,
And after a drop of firewater
You loved a good row.
"Brings me alive," you said.
Once, when we were at it,
You leaned forward,
And they went, your teeth.
They dropped, wobbled,
Loosed into a huge leer,
Madly at odds with your wrath.
I wished I could have laughed.

I stood in the chill of that chapel,
To view the stiffened wreckage you'd become.
Your face peeped from the coffin's plush,
An Ophelia who'd had her span,
But just as dead among the weeds.
And there it was,
That same inane grin,
The ghost of that dental mishap.
They must have popped them in
Just before we arrived.
I wished I could have laughed.

Tony Hudd, Margate, Kent

FOR MUSIC

in the dizzy rain
the light of your hair gleams
green as the snow
on the frill of the kerb
stone: loneliness croons by
the street-lamp bending
down distance; listening to light
as she swims the sky
around and throws the rain
about; grinning I ask myself
does this ring, does this ring
or am I just banging on the moon?

Zibiah Alfred, Orpington, Kent

SONNET

There's no trace of you anywhere:
No glint of earring under the bed,
No smell, no taste of your hair
In my mouth. Emptiness instead.

There's no letter wedging a drawer,
No colour left on the walls.
No need to wonder what it was for
Or whether to avoid your calls.

The sofa is clear of crumbs now,
Leaving nothing of you behind.
The air is still of why's and how's
And the words we couldn't find.

New dust falls in your absence,
Filling my mouth with silence.

Sue Aylward, Ramsgate, Kent

A NOMAD

Where can I lay my head tonight
A wandering?
On grassy knoll or wayside green
A softening.
I have no walls of thick dark stone
A sheltering.
But I may go where-e'er I please
Meandering.
Up mountain pass or through the glen
A trekking.
And I will stop by pool and stream
A paddling.
Across the sun-baked desert sand
A sinking.
Or through the forest green
A shading.
And when my roaming days are o'er
A resting.
I'll lay my head on God's good earth
A sleeping.

Helen D Thompson, Longfield, Kent

THIS MOMENT

In sage contemplation, Harry the hamster stares
And the music from a distant TV spars with
Occasional laughter from a bedroom upstairs
That rodent doesn't run, but ponders from his wheel
He and I are both thinking how
This day of butter sunshine has run through our hands

My daughter's laughter and her portrait of Harry hang
Around his cage in this room where the old slate clock
ticks
But doesn't gong anymore
I step over my son's lego starship in the darkness
That clock needs winding

But the hamster and I are wondering if I don't
And instead open its glass door and catch that pendulum
Can I just stop this time business
This unspeakably precious passing of seconds
And forcibly hold on to this moment like a long, aching
breath

Mark Holihan, Broadstairs, Kent

DAUGHTER

She comes back into my life like a whirlwind,
And when she has gone,
I look round the house to see what is missing.
My new lipstick, a CD and my heart.

Teresa Baker, Tonbridge, Kent

JUST A CHILD'S MARBLE

This morning I found a world
As I walked through my woods.
Muddied, among the leaf loam and new bluebell grass,
White opaque glass swirled with clear blues.

I remembered how they fascinated me.
Different sizes had different names;
Now forgotten.
Whirls of livid rainbow stories
Trapped in hard smoothness.

This morning's find was battered and dull.
I washed it in the spring stream.
Rubbed it with wishes,
Held it up to the sunlight.
It shone briefly
As the stream drops at the ends of my fingers
Glisten.

Liz Dawes, Speldhurst, Kent

STAPLER

The hand span of a long, hard man,
Rigid and cold and matt and black.

Yawning jaws - angular, smooth -
Host to a slender metal tongue,
A ribbed band of sallow steel.

Stands. Snaps shut.
Top gum punches bottom;
Out spit tiny, silvery fangs.

Allison Carvalho, East Ham, Greater London

NUMBERS

When I watch the news I fear numbers.
Numbers fall like snow and cover all with nothing.
I fear countdowns that make wars like flowers,
And missiles delicate as match flames.

I fear anniversaries and birthdays marching
To the rim of nothing.

I fear numbers in columns, like stock market indices,
In columns like bills and advancing troops.

Numbers, they are marching towards you.
Look at them in rows, like a death mask smile,
Or rows of tombstones.
They look at you and tell you the truth;
No illusions now, no wavering
And no dreams. We've got you.

Michael Brett, Palmers Green, Greater London

WHAT SHALL WE DO TODAY?

Let's run out in the street
And assert our rights,
Whatever they may be.

Let's stop working
For one glorious day,
Just for the hell of it.

Let us paint placards -
"Down with everything."
"You're not doing that in my name."

Then wave at the press
As we're carted away,
Have our fifteen minutes of fame.

It would be fun, wouldn't it,
Make quite a change
From the humdrum of our existence?

Okay, you stay here,
I'll go on my own.
Now, where did I put my bus pass?

Sandra Curtin, Sunbury-on-Thames, Greater London

THE SECRET-SHARERS

By tomorrow night
The neighbours
May
Be back

By tomorrow night
The spies
May have found
Our lair

By tomorrow night
Our passions
May
Be spent

But, oh
Till then,
My love
Till then.

Solomon Odeleye, London

AT THE OTHER END OF THE NIGHT

Somewhere at the other end of the night
You are sleeping
While I am lying in the dark
Imagining your peaceful face
And the gentle breathing of your body
And your heavy hair
On the pillow.

Somewhere at the other end of the night
You are sleeping
While I am lying in the dark, smiling
And listening to the beating of my heart
While it breaks.

Susanne Kermani, Neasden, Greater London

OPERA AT IFORD

Elegiac evening.
Suspend time and disbelief;
Cast, costumed,
Haunt the lawns and terraces.
Music has all the permanence
Of a ghost.
I pinch myself and sit behind the wheel,
Bound by keys and signposts,
Motorways, tomorrow.
But then I raise my eyes and see
Above the shadow of the combe
Some careless god has spilt
His cup of stars
And left them strewn across the knap of heaven.

Charles Johnston, London

MEMORY OF YESTERDAY

On a cold autumnal evening
I awake like a festered wound
Of old voices, echoes of the past
Trapped in the darkness
Of your dwindling face.

The contours of a mirror's mirage
Of dancing shadow boxers
Wavering their shoulders
Like the wings of drowning butterflies
Are my memories, whispering
With a mouth moulded like a bleeding snail.

The moon is nothing but a silvery bladder
Filled with festered blood and lost voices;
Falling into the night, I dream of a
Blood-red bridge hanging above
The ashes and abysses of the deserter's flight,
Leading back into the dawning landscape
Where we were still together.

Eli Park Sorensen, Camden, Greater London

A VISITOR

"Do you remember me?" she asked,
Standing at my front door.
"I sat at the back of your class:
You taught me to draw.

"I was the one who wore braces,
Who wasn't good at sums.
I couldn't do up me laces,
And I sucked me thumbs.

"Never remembered me spellings,
And writing was a chore.
But you made my life compelling:
You taught me to draw.

"Was useless at sports and running,
Couldn't catch a ball, if I tried.
But soon I learned to be cunning,
That's how I survived.

"Now I'm designing dresses,
So, in spite of all me flaws,
It's to you I send me blessings:
You taught me to draw."

Jane Willis, Stanmore, Greater London

FOUR SHORT WORDS

"Six months at most," he quietly muttered
Incoherently I stuttered, disoriented, numb
My flowing tears I fought.

With ground-eating steps I rushed for home
Head bowed, all alone
The laughter of strangers seemed thunderously loud
I, enveloped in a darkened cloud.

Stars twinkled as if to mock my now-shortened view
A vapour trail hung suspended as if to taunt my own
despair.

Courting couples walked side by side
Parents with children and shopping abide.

Huddled, alone, vague and bereft
Angry at their purposeful step
I wept.

No, this could not be happening to me
Turn back that clock, erase those words
Set me free.

Gloria Hargreaves, Shepperton, Greater London

INTANGIBLE

I have a hidden cross,
Its secret it will keep,

Lashes me
Through the roads,

People I encounter -
Bus advertisements.

My cross knows me
Alone

And I know it.

Hannah Kelly, London

TOUGH AUDIENCE

They said Monday's audience would be tough,
Blaming the rain, so I start with the Englishman,
The Scotsman and the sheep from Pontypridd,
Which is normally a knockout.

You can measure the silence in octaves, so
I try the Tom Jones song and flounder in
The high C's, while the mother-in-law jokes
Trip over political correctness.

Last resort, I do a pratfall and break a leg,
Which sometimes happens. Now my leg becomes
Their funny bone. They rise to applaud me,
Just like the old days, while outside the rain
Is washing my name from the posters.

Peter Butler, Chiswick, Greater London

CAFÉ POEM

Poems are for pavement cafés
Where cigarette ends mark
Each cut and thrust
Of thought and tongue
While coffee hot as
Passionate argument
Warms the blood
And the dazzle of sun
Ferments our thoughts
Like wine.
We are alive
Here in the light
Here with the aroma of good things,
Relaxing in an ocean of ideas.
Glimpsing horizons
But content
With the timeless pleasure
Of this moment.

Lynette Bishop, Acton, Greater London

STATIONARY

I met my love at the station
In the town of poor excuse
And the train we caught
Was on platform nought
And bound for not in use.

And we sat as the land stood past us
By the click of the cancelled clock,
And we rattled our joints
On the frozen points
In the discontinued stock.

For time is an ageing commodity,
It powered the enactment of dreams,
Our forefathers mined it,
Our fathers refined it,
And little remains in the seams.

And I threatened to love her till Wednesday
And Tuesday and Monday as well,
And the sun went clunk
And the dark was drunk
And we held each other like hell.

Alan Franks, Richmond, Surrey

ACTING DEBUT

Today I touched the sun
And the heat spread through me,
Scorched the core of asbestos
Pieces of me built by the pains of the years
Safely tucked away - protected.
Today it melted and left me free
No need for caution.
Today I touched the sun.

Today I reached the stars
Today I became someone else
Felt her pain, knew her love,
Gave her to you
And you drank in her every word,
Laughed with her, sighed with her,
Held her to you and understood her.
Today I touched the stars.

Patricia Taylor, Woking, Surrey

URBAN FOX

When sometimes you pause
In your easy gait
Between here and there
In my garden
And give the house
A long, considering stare,
I, behind glass,
Watch with a quickened heart
Trying to catch
Before you part,
The essence of your being,
Knowing I never shall.

You are elusive
As cloud shadow
Passing over wheat,
Yet wise enough
To recognise
How wildly
The human heart can beat.

Michael Tanner, Guildford, Surrey

LOVERS

Tonight we got rid of the car,
Instead, we took the bus
And we swooshed to the cinema,
To re-discover us.

It was just as we were, before,
When we were young and keen,
When kisses and cuddles meant more,
Than what was on the screen.

And since nostalgia can be
A pensioner's delight,
The film we decided to see,
Was old, and black and white.

We settled in seats at the back,
Where love can writhe and leap,
But just as we leaned to attack,
We both zoomed off to sleep.

John Dove, Rustington, Sussex

MIRROR

There were days in my distant youth
When I could not take my eyes off her,
Even sought her in her natural habitat,
In lakes and rainpools, in the eyes of lovers.

It was not just vanity, but proof
Of my existence, when I felt invisible,
Confronted by a world of frightening reality.
The familiar reflection comforted.

My mirror's memory is long, but she
Does not re-run the past; soft focus and nostalgia.
She is greedy with her trophies, gloats over new
Flaws, is nigardly with compliments.

Insidious, she nibbles at the contours,
Dissolving structure and solidity,
Eroding, loosening the line, a drawing
Left out in the rain.

Perhaps one day she'll swallow me, like Alice,
Retaining just her empty shining self, hanging
Complacent, undisturbed, until her silvering decays,
Fragments, like her memory - and mine.

Mary Smythe, Swanborough, Lewes, Sussex

LIFE SENTENCE

For most of us
The lives we lead fall
Short of expectation.

The prize we strive
For glitters brighter
Than the bits of tin we win.

The vision of the architect
Becomes the concrete building block
Of his disappointment.

Stories we dream freeze dry
To granules of instant dust
Before we finish writing them,

As though the craft of piling
Word on insubstantial word
Is not creation but reduction.

A single sentence holds such promise
Until we come to finish it.

William Wood, Etchingham, Sussex

THE SEASHORE

The seductive curves of hills and trees,
Far in the distance, beckon to me,
But they never win, on a sunny day,
Here by the seashore, I have to stay.

With sighing surf and rolling shingle,
Clean fresh air, make senses tingle,
Shimmering sand, reflects the sun,
Background noises of laughter and fun.

But come the autumn, all brown and gold,
The seductive curves become more bold,
No longer faithful I cannot resist,
The hills and trees and morning mists.

C J Bolesworth, Littlehampton, Sussex

FALSE SMILE

It started like stealth
Moving, plunging
Outwards from the centre
Digging through the ice
Like a ship in a frozen sea.

The edges of the mouth
Almost reaching the ears, now,
And the rectangles of teeth
Like dirty windows.

The performance over
The curtains close
And the eye's mist
Creeps over.

Vanessa Burgar, Chichester, Sussex

THE MAN I MET LAST NIGHT

Awake now;
Day begins
Sifting the night
Sifting yesterday
Sifting dreams
That for these few moments
Are more real
Than the day.

Those I met
The angels sent me
From the future,
From the past,
Some from a realm
I don't yet know.
I hope I meet him
In this world;
The man I met last night.

Lesley Murray, East Grinstead, Sussex

THE VIEW FROM ST MARY'S

I rented a view: monochromic sunset,
Silky crinkled harbour spread with acquiescent boats;
Jacks spilt across a playground.

On the hill, cottages receded into dusk until
Tiny windows pierced the dark like angry insects
And the rain advanced.

A predator's shadow, crouched on the horizon
Watched a boat depart, its crown a single light
To fish "in peril on the sea."

A dapple-grey rowing boat, oars safely inside,
Bucked at its rope as a cloud battalion charged
Upon the drowsy islands.

Invading quiet skies, storm raised its roar,
Raged a short lifespan. Calm brought forgetfulness.
The sleepy rowing boat, oars tucked

Inside its belly, nodded on the rope.
Time darkened. Like a ghost behind my eyelids,
The image floated momentarily, faded like a memory.

Catherine Rose, Ickwell, Bedfordshire

MIA'S FIRST RAINBOW

Hours are ours to fill as we choose
Or lose.
How long does the sun take to rise
Above the sea - red golfball
On an instant's tee?
Does a rainbow last an hour?
Or outlast a shower?
Mia stands transfixed at the open door;
"Pink - yellow - top of sky."
First small poem from childish eye.
Hours are ours to muse or lose.

Robin Edgar, Bedford, Bedfordshire

BREEDING GROUND

The people erred.
He sent flood.
They rebelled again. He sent frogs,
locusts, blood, putrefaction, viruses;
insatiable in appetite,
tiny and infinite as darkness.
The people suffered,
recovered, erred
again, headlong, splendid.

So he favoured them, sent them oils,
medicines, machines; spilt the secrets
of the corn, the skies, the turning water, the hills.
Prosperity, and increase. Plagues
they suffered no more. Visible from the outermost
heaven spawning in their tide of high territories
they were insatiable
in appetite, infinite and
tiny as darkness.

Adrian Lenthall, Leighton Buzzard, Bedfordshire

THE DISTANT CRY

Maybe I heard you amidst the cries
In shades of golden sunset
You were the shadows
Amidst the rocky fronts in the distant land

You followed me to oceans deep
And there you held my hand
We sat together
In silence and the world softly smiled

An inward wave did sweep you up the shore
I felt your soft padded paw
It stole a frozen tear
your sweetest voice I then did hear

How we did sing in harmony
In the darkness of the night
And I mistook your tender cry
In the deserts place alone

You told me not to mourn
Your whisper it did soothe me
You followed me and there we walked
Across the deep dark shore

Tracy Jane Briggs, Ascot, Berkshire

GHOST SHIP

I could sail a ship; send it foam-breaking
To the greatest rogues of the deep.

Across brave waves my sails would fly,
Like thunder-heads on this world's rim; riding

The spray of each crest. Sketch its wake
By stars that chink like the bright mail

Of my armour; the last gasps and bursts of heroes
That sink, are sucked to this black-holing night;
Become myths before ever
My sun's fierce pride
First burned.

And my ship,
As brave to this sea as stars to the night, its bowsprit
Shall carry the last rage of the sunset
Like a maiden,
A goddess.

Gareth Roberts, Newbury, Berkshire

WITHOUT YOU

I can hear the ticking of the clock,
The slow beating of my heart,
The breathing of the wood of my desk.
Apart from you I exist in a vacuum,
Suspended where the wheels of time
Rotate as slowly as thick old treacle falls from a spoon.
I reach out tentatively to push them forward
To the glorious time when we will
Lie naked together again.

Gail Wisbey, Windsor, Berkshire

GOODBYE

Stepping out onto the winding road.
That draws us ever onward.
Parting forever as star-crossed lovers,
The hope is pulling us forward.
What will I find? I do not know,
My thoughts I try to cast.
To find out just what lies in front,
Good riddance to the past.
I'm striding out onto the trail,
And the years will fly and fly.
Then I'll look back with no remorse,
On the last of my goodbyes.

Richard James, Caversham, Reading, Berkshire

THE QUARREL

Closed hard face
Not a flicker of compassion
For the turmoil which resides like a hard stone
In my breast

He sits statue-like
Face turned uncompromisingly
Towards the flickering screen
Blinkered to the here and now

Will we be speaking
By the time the day is out?
Not at this rate
The silence is like an impenetrable fog

As if to make things worse
The rain tumbles out of a leaden sky
The plants lift their faces
Where are some golden drops for me?

Ruth Tietjens, Crowthorne, Berkshire

MIDDLE YEARS

April, and all the trees that just before
Had looked too old, too greyed, too brittle
To bend with the supple ease of youth, now
Stand in mists of gentle green, leaves so small,
So finely formed, yet their clouded
Multitudes are of such an entity
To challenge all the vaunted beauty nature
Can display.

And I am jealous of this hallowed time
That brings to mind the sunlit days and once
Imagined immortality of youth
And I would grasp and hold fast this fleeting
Time that makes such imagination real,
Even to the forgetting that with June
Maturity will shroud leaves darker green
And with the turning of the year lead them
Fallen, captive to autumn, winter and
To fear.

Mike Wilkinson, Burghfield Common, Berkshire

A ROOM AT THE INN

That night we dined on guinea fowl and wine,
And finished with a soufflé smooth as sin.
Miranda, when I held your hand in mine
You stole my soul and crept beneath my skin.
Do you remember an inn?

The waiter murmured, soft in candlelight,
I kissed you, tilting up your heart-shaped chin,
We were Miranda, for one spellbound night,
Lovers like Columbine and Harlequin.
Do you remember an inn?

Our love affair flared up then turned to ash,
A flaming catherine wheel in fizzing spin,
Illicit passion always doomed to crash,
But oh, Miranda, how my soul's grown thin.
Do you remember an inn?

Tamsin Forman, Brill, Buckinghamshire

MY FATHER'S HAND

My father's hand in mine,
Thick, strong fingers,
Short for such a massive palm -
A doer's, maker's, hand.
The spade-like nails as neat as ever.

So many years since this grown-up boy
Stopped holding daddy's hand,
That old comfortable glove
Of boundless strength
Is still so much larger than mine.

I try to reassure
My father's hand,
As it shakes gently
In his closing illness.

Nigel Lambert, Milton Keynes, Buckinghamshire

SAD MARGARET

Sad Margaret laughed full joyfully
With her fellow guests as she shared her joke
And drained her second glass of dinner wine,
Then filled a moment's silence with
An amusing anecdote.

She did not notice the brief and embarrassed
Exchange of glances
They did not notice the introspection lying
Deep within her eyes.

Returning to her lonely room
In sparkling sandals and defiant scarlet dress
She enjoyed again the startled admiration
She saw in other guests.

Once there she poured
Her final drink of the day,
And prepared for the night, expensive pills and lotions
Close to hand - those designed to hold truth at bay.

Thus ready, she rehearsed her breakfast time lines
Then sought the silent solace of dreamless sleep.

Elizabeth Savage, Wantage, Oxfordshire

IT WILL BE SILENT NOW

It will be silent now.

The trees have stilled their metal-hard roots that quest
In search of new life, like settlers finding new land.

The earth is turning, under the sun and under the plough,
And each day new wonders unfold and fade.

The leaves have turned into life-size golden replicas, each
Tiny vein fossilised as if in stone. They fall, the drifting dry
Wings, carriages from which miracles can be witnessed.

For a time the earth will still, turning only under the sun,
and
For a time the mother of all will wait, her patience endless
As eternity.

Cold fingers of the frost will return to their reign,
fashioning ice-beautiful pictures with frozen streams.
The northern winds will sweep down over the land,
Another invasion from the endless wastelands,
And for a season, there will be silence.

In place of the leaves the snow will fall, and in place of the
Chestnut the ice will form.

This is a temporary death.

Miranda Latham-Jackson, Oxford, Oxfordshire

THE DISUSED RAILWAY

The station platform remained; we waited there
Like Muscovites in army coats, expecting snow.
The winter dell and disused track seemed perfect
For disturbance, the improbable a simple act
Of will. We loitered as the day defaulted,
Defying induction, awaiting trains.

When snow came, its flakes furred our boots.
The old rails were presently erased,
Each sleeper stolen, resolves
Obliterated. Though we remained,
We knew there would be no more trains.

Siobhan Dowd, West Oxford, Oxfordshire

HEAT

I sleep to the hiss of heat
As it slinks across my room
Seducing me to slumber

And when I wake
Immobile with warmth
Lying idle
Hearing
Hot water pulsing
As it courses through house veins,
I feel the heat within and all around me
And know I have been tempted too far
By the hot hiss at my ear

One flick of the switch
And then
Let there be heat

Catherine Lofthouse, Borehamwood, Hertfordshire

AUTUMN SOUNDS

An autumn whisper
Golden leaves crisp on the ground
My children jump in.

The leaf murmur
My child hears for the first time
With his hearing aid.

Those brown and red leaves
A boy's small hand crumbles them
A cry of delight.

Hillary Taylor, Harpenden, Hertfordshire

SOUTHAMPTON WATER

All day it has rained across the stout hills
Along the coast and out onto sluggish swells
Where we watch through small portholes
Other boats, floating like soft warm pillows.

It is not so much that it rains all day
More that there's nothing to do but wait
Wait until time allows other elements
To open a route for the sun's appearance.

For now, we watch as it continues
To smudge the harbour into smeared grey hues
Contented by the creaks our water-bound
Home makes. Until the sun drowns the rain out.

Liz Marzano, Andover, Hampshire

REPRISE

Smouldering fires burn autumn leaves,
Smoke billowing, drifting on high,
As each season interweaves.

The long days pass. Your heart deceives
Like the shade of a butterfly.
Smouldering fires burn autumn leaves.

An Indian summer the weather reprieves,
Not a cloud in the clear blue sky.
As each season interweaves.

The heat is gone, the grey mist grieves,
Murmuring winter's lullaby
Smouldering fires burn autumn leaves.

Father time, the old year bereaves,
His sickle held on high.
As each season interweaves.

Through each dark night my heart retrieves
The peace that has passed me by.
Smouldering fires burn autumn leaves
As each season, interweaves.

Freya Bryant, Southampton, Hampshire

IDYLL BY THE AVON AT FORDINGBRIDGE

There is pleasure here
That summer calls forth
From children playing on mown grass

By cool waters running
Between the old bridge parapets
Where the brown trout pass

As coot and swan
Glide on by
Beneath a cloudless azure sky

To the sound of leather
On willow bat
As voices cry: "How's that?"

Echo across the rippling stream
Where anglers
Cast their rods and dream

Not of the one
That got away
But of the gentle sunny day

Liz Hanson, Fordingbridge, Hampshire

BLUES

Red is her colour - not subtle like the rust-tinted sun
Slipping into the sea, but strumpet-red,
Vulgar, intrusive,
Loud, abusive;
Blood red - sucking the life out of a marriage.

Black is his colour - dyed-black thinning hair,
Moused, gelled and spiked in some last-chance salon -
Out of his mind
Purblind;
Too far out to ever find his way back.

Grey is Jamie's colour; school-uniform grey, sock grey -
hold my hand tightly grey -
Seven-year-old grey-speckled eyes
Clouding over in hurt surprise
At things he can't understand.

My colour is blue, betrayed blue,
A blow to the heart from out of the blue -
A low-down blues blue
Metallic blue -
The birthday present he drove down the drive and out of
my life.

Laurie Reeves, Southampton, Hampshire

FIRST INKLINGS

Disillusion and untruths
Lie in a puddle of tears.
Damp footsteps lead away
Down the dark corridor of sorrow
Out onto the soft beach
Where lost lovers go
To wade in deeper waters
Until the past is made bearable
Or forgotten.

The lonely heart toils slowly on its way
Midst torrid canyons, thorny briars and chasms.
The lonely heart might sometimes wish to play
But finds that playing alone is dull; fears banish spasms

Of mild delight when others linger near,
And are bridged by endless days of lonely labour.

The world in pairs winds slowly.

Jan Peters, Rookley, Isle of Wight

*South
West*

THE BEACH

Gazing at the sun as it begins to melt into the horizon,
On a late September afternoon.
I listen to the crashing of the waves against the rocks
As I sit upon a silk sand dune.
Sinking my feet into a deep hole
Into the cool, smooth, buttercup sand.
I watch the tide come in, the aquarium blue waves
Replace the tired out land.
Blankets of golden orange and deep velvet reds
Lay pleasantly soft in the sky.
Squawking seagulls, scavenge for scraps of food
With pierced eyes as they fly by.
Fresh seawater salt lays finely upon my lips
Bedding itself on my skin.
The beach is my own paradise
A picture of nature's many beautiful things.
Daylight begins to slowly evaporate.
The ashen evening sky slowly starts to appear
Winds gradually begin to strengthen
An unwelcome reminder that winter is drawing near.

Kerry Thompson, Yeovil, Somerset

SWAN

His beak's a whittled
Carrot hammered home
Under the harlequin mask and the brow's fierce pain

His neck, a meat-hook
Gloved in polar velvet
Melts and bends in the frost-fire of his spirit

With whiteness whisked
As stiff as a roast ghost
With sudden

Wingclatter and angry admonishments
Of the flossed-up tail
Loudly he upbraids the elements

Till (water and sky
Put firmly in their place)
He composes himself to float with a galleon's grace

Anthony Watts, Taunton, Somerset

I KNOW A PLACE

Where the forest keeps me safe
And the bough is my protector
Here, the grassy bank is my pillow
On which I dream a fairytale sleep
Giant red toadstools are my bedstead
Their spots twinkling nightlights in my room

Midnight blooms forget me not
Delicate brave blue petals see all
Whilst woodland friends watch over me
Listening out for danger's creep
Mice, rabbits and somewhere beneath
The dense fur of moles forms my underlay

The sovereign moon looks on
Half hidden through picket trunks
As I rest at last my bone-weary limbs
Happy in slumber, fearless and deep
Until that silvery path shies of my face
Let me lie still - I know a place

Simon Le Merle, Radstock, Somerset

HOMECOMING

In my shoes I carry sand
From all the beaches of the world
And pollen brushed from flowers in strange places.
In my eyes is the light of dawns and sunsets,
Days born and dying over far horizons.
Through my hair has blown the winds of land and sea.
Now my feet walk the pathway to your door,
Past English flowers in a quiet garden.
In my eyes love dawns again,
After a night of forgetting,
And your touch on my hair.

Graham Jennings, Banwell, Somerset

THE SUICIDE

Wild west wind bends the sedge
Dying by the river
We cut him down
The man who hung himself
After years of screaming "voices"
And nameless infected darkness

The stream runs creamy afoam with mud
Bearing the pain away
Of dabbling in the whirlpool of his madness
We were afraid
His legacy
Our guilt

Fiona Hiern-Cooke, Bishops Lydeard, Somerset

THE LESSON

Think hard about this scene
Observe the goat
Pick agile ways along the mountain rim

Look closely at the tree
Absorb the bird
Thrilling the baby with his blissful song

Look deeply in the pool
Discern the fish
Flick darting fire among the lotuses

Goat's grace, bird's song, bright fins
Branch not yet broken, water not yet gone,
The warp and weft of someone's other world

Dark thunder rolls away beyond the mountain
Goat and bird, baby, fish, all done
Thin threads, soft bones, small prices
To be paid

This place is not material to the plan
It lies in line of fire

A war is being won

Susan Boyle, Bath, Somerset

THE OLD COACH ROAD

Behind me
The fleeing horsemen race
On hidden paths
Across the haunted hills

The mediaeval way
Still peopled by the shadows
Stirs itself
As deer lift silent feet

And in the sky
The buzzard sways
Whose gimlet eyes reach out
To pierce the tottering lamb

Yet still beneath the leaves
The quivering ferns await
The packhorse, that will not
Pass this way again

Suzanne Henslow, Nether Stowey, Somerset

DAD IS ASKING FOR YOU

Dad, when did you get so old
Both your lumpy old hands
On top of your briefcase, you're now ready
To go

She got you ready really
For me to collect you
Your important son, as promised, has come
Tables have turned on you

How fragile your face looks
Ready to cry, like a withered leaf
Your big shocked milky eyes say
Help me

How easy was it to accept that first
Wheelchair ride
The piss-bottle pride
That kneeling chat

Now I still listen respectfully
But in charge as I hoist you
Around the room
Like a rag doll

Michael FitzGerald, Jersey, Channel Islands

PURRRR

A cold dark day:
A dark room in the process of renovation,
With a bare concrete floor.
Used as a storeroom for building materials,
It looks nothing like a comfortable living room.
But there is a fire burning,
Throwing out heat and the orange glow of flames,
To the cold, jumbled room.
In front of the fire, on a piece of cardboard
Sits a pale ginger cat,
Eyes half-closed in enjoyment of the heat,
Soaking in and savouring the warmth and glow.
Utter comfort.

Lesley Steadman, Lydney, Gloucestershire

THE CALAIS ROAD

This is sad country,
horizon a long, long sigh
encircling endless pale fields -
squads of trees signal silently.

There - and there again -
a low walled enclosure
a tall cross
a crop of white stones,
neat, orderly, military.

Grey weeping sky long since
leeched this blood-soaked earth.
No rain, no wind, can erase the echo
of that Somme-scream
from this exhausted place.

Jacqueline Dench, Gloucester, Gloucestershire

AFTERMATH

I thought I'd run
Barefoot on cold and crumbling,
Damp, brown soil,
Press mouldering leaves and thorns
Against my breast
And batter fists against
Erected barriers of the mind
Or yowl to the winds.
But even in the night my body,
Uninhabited, lies calm.
I yearn to cry releasing tears,
Dammed, withered, seared,
They stay at my demand.

You ask me how I feel, while
Not wanting to hear,
Wrap me in empathetic kindness
Knowing how I should act.
I fear the softly, speaking smile.
It may disarm my frail defence
And I shall drown.

Christine Wisdom, Cheltenham, Gloucestershire

BELLA'S GAME

Bella opened with a gambit
"It's time we had a little drink."

Wine and conversation flowed,
Compliments filtered through cigarette smoke.

Proposed double meaning toasts
Were exchanged for kisses.

Skilful moves prompted
A stratagem of accidental touching.

A subtly-introduced second bottle
Stimulated the middle game.

Soft lights and love songs
With compulsory dancing.

Unsteady steps became a smooch.
The sacrifice: "It's getting late."

Preceded: "One for the road."
Coffee laced with a dash of brandy.

This farewell ritual was repeated
Before Bella's end-game manoeuvre.

"You'd better stay."
Check and mate Bella.

Les Merton, Redruth, Cornwall

SONG

On the warm, warm hearth of my heart
There flames a song,
Born of the wild winter wind
And the ravishing rain.
A lay for high heroes
And the righting of wrong,
And lone, lone women,
Climbing their towers of pain:

When the lilies in the wormwood
Have ceased their calling,
And the last, long tear is over and shed.
When the blessing of the morning
Oh so gently is falling
On all the weary childer abed.
Soft to your side will I then be stealing,
With fume of thyme your soul to be sealing,
Joy and love and the peace of healing.

John Gordon, Penzance, Cornwall

LAVINIA MAUD

The old woman lay on the trolley
white hair-haloed,
her face like a crescent moon.
Beside her machinery hummed and blipped,
screens glowed restless neon green.
Beyond, the siren fitfully screamed
"That's it, can you hear me darlin'?
You've broken your hip.
We'll take you up to the ward,
do you hear me love?"
Lavinia Maud 1909
F263057
lay under the glare and cellular blanket,
a shallow imprint on canvas,
a drifted pebble on sand,
her shell filled with light,
dreaming of white lace and rosebuds.

Veronica Ferry, Poole, Dorset

SHE CAME BACK

For months she held her peace
crafty minx
then she came waltzing back into my life unbidden
her precious gift of words
That trip over themselves;
Written on anything that comes to hand
The back of an envelope.
A scrap of torn paper
What unblocked the vent
Like a cork from a bottle?
A young man untimely taken
his family torn apart in grief
The relief of welcoming her back into my life
sets my heart singing

Brenda Smith, Gillingham, Dorset

TO THE PERFECT GUY

You're just around the bend
It's said,
I could find you any time

Maybe
If I lean against the wall
You'll amble around the swerve

Life is rushing by
While I'm waiting
For the perfect guy

I can't wait forever
For you to stroll around
My corner

Alice Fergie, Verwood, Dorset

BEDBOROUGH BY NIGHT

Sound resounds like hollow crates.
The echoing night reverberates,
To milkers' drum beats, dispensing cake.
Continuous crashing shake.
The gardens merge into the dark,
Where shadow forms move between leaf and bark.
The black bats flitter-flatter on leathery wings.
In the distance the ringroad sings.
The farm house creaks and groans,
Cracking old bones.
The still night heaves a sigh.
The wind carrying the shrill cry;
The hunting owl,
The vixen's growl,
The heifer's calving push,
The cat underneath the bush.
And the rusted-out garden gate,
Squeaks eerily to its mate,
Which swings in the parlour yard,
Where the moon stands guard.

Paula Langdon, Wimborne, Dorset

ELIZABETHAN GHOSTS

My bedroom is where
Horses slept. Through my
Window Elizabethan ghosts
Carry armfuls of wool to
The ships on the river today
Silt dry. Even Raleigh as a
Boy trod these lanes, the
Local pub his only memorial.

Now the stable is yuppie red
Brick. Owned by a nurse and
An artist. One injects, one pastel
Smudges, neither wool-weave.
No history. I look out of my window.
Post offices, chalked playgrounds,
Bus stops and double yellow lines
Segregate village from villager.

But Elizabethan ghosts still
Walk through these walls.

Morwenna Griffiths, East Budleigh, Devon

HOW WIDE THE SKIES

Stretching polished black
Overhead, cloudless
Scattered with astral diamonds
To the world's edge

So remote
Yet just another highway
For our restless race to roam
Now that none can spare the time
To walk the world

Just another litter bin
For worn-out space probes
And the clutter
Of scientists' expensive efforts
To claim the universe

And yet, from here
What distant star-decked beauty

How wide the skies

Jacqui Fogwill, Tavistock, Devon

SEASONED EBONY GRAIN

From seasoned ebony grain. Tap, tap,
With disciplined hands
And tools honed sharp,
He carves a pulsing purple vein,
In maiden neck as satin smooth.
He thinks a slip could leave her dead. Tap, tap.
Life's sap would find her fondled breast
To slowly seep on secret curves,
Engraved in memory, blest.

As he makes his chase. Tap, tap.
And searches reassurance in her face,
Her dark brown eyes seem moist with tears,
Her lips appear to smile,
Or so he would maintain.
Then he reasons with style. Tap, tap,
No woman ever was so loved,
As she from seasoned ebony grain.

Brigid Gibbs, Tiverton, Devon

THE LIBRARY

I am lost again.
Embedded deep with this peaceful palace,
Facing a firewall of fact and fiction
Driven up by artists and wordsmiths
Unaware that their thoughtful imaginings
Would become the foundations of this place.

Silently, as there is no other way,
I become a drowning handful of sand.
Drunk on my love of other people's dreams,
Enveloped by the sound of thinking,
The hum of pictures behind all these strangers' eyes.

There can be no better plain, than that of thought.
One that throws wide the beauty of all the places
Where time stands still for someone else.

There is nothing so intoxicating
As the endless pews of promise
In this church of words.

Sarah Bailey, Exeter, Devon

JANUARY'S DEVON

I see you Devon
The weather rampaging across your desolate landscape.
Delicate hedge, row after row
Pummelled and fought.
Every crevice thick with the muddy mixture
And the trees are awake
Their sinister moaning
Breaks across the expanse to no-one listening.

Today there are no romantic heather-filled dips or rises.
Sky moving with anger, earthwards descending.
Each stile seems to cry: "Onwards. Feel how alone you can
be."
And I sense the dangerous isolation
In each slippery gate and hidden burrow.

Through thick soles and double socks
You soak my feet with thoughtless drops
As I stomp home along the same old tracks.
Until your bashful apology; when grey gives way to watery
light
And every puddle is a chalice filled with sky.

Laura Bolt, Ivybridge, Devon

SURVIVOR'S SONG

We who can soar
Eagle-hearted and high
Beyond all projections

We who can soar
And dance with the angels
On cloud swirls of splendour
Knowing the truth
Is a feeling of starlight

We who can dance
And make light of the darkness
And yield with the crushing
Of dreams in the dawn light

And spin love out of nothing
But damp earth and sunbeams

We who can join
Join together in spirit
And weave gossamer circles
In air full of failings

We who can soar

Paula Kovacs, Sandford, Crediton, Devon

TO THE CHURCH

Everyone had gone.
The house was silent as the car drew up.
August - so hot;
Too hot for finery.
I picked up my bouquet
You put on your top hat.
We were nervous - our hands were shaking.
"Ready?" you said.
We left the house together
For the church.

Everyone was there.
We all fell silent as the car drew up.
August - so hot;
Too hot for black.
I stared at the wreath
They'd put above you.
I was nervous - my legs were shaking.
"Ready?" someone said.
We left the house together
For the very last time.

Janet Beardsall, Ottery St Mary, Devon

STATUESQUE

You are night.
Moonlight's silver empowers you.
Encircled by stars, you smile statuesque;
Your marble face unbroken,
Your cool eyes unblinking,
Your chiselled lips unyielding.

The first crack of sun splits open frozen hills;
Its warmth cascading onto rich, brown soil.

The fiery glow enlivens a soft procession of trees;
Single grey leaves melting to warm green.

A solitary oak shakes off the night's chill;
Frosted veil lifts to reveal rich, red hues.

The bright blue sky hides nothing.
The earth stirs easily from the sun's touch.
Here daylight's colours embrace me,
As I wrap myself in the warmth
You leave untouched.

Charlie Fisher, Totnes, Devon

TODDLER AT THE TATE

Wish the Mondrians were a climbing frame
Get all those colours on my finger tips,
Then roll across Rothko's purple plain
And take my first steps at Leger's Circus.
See my face in glass, glaze and bronze,
Roll once more on Rothko's purple and beyond.
Slap my hands on the floor,
Head down, my noise keeps time
Till I come to "stop right there" shoe shine.
And look up to a security guard's face,
Who offers a hanky for my sudden tears.
I cry, and colours are tumbling towers
Then daddy calms me
While a flying magnolia passes by
Made from the hanky in my hand.

Sarah Buckland, Exmouth, Devon

THE EMPTY HOUSE

I savour a silence sometimes
That I can taste and swallow
And still hear how the fridge hums.
A silence where breakfast TV
Has been swept away,
Along with the morning's crumbs.

A silence, where no-one
Asks for anything and the cushions
Stay asleep and sound
And a bird outside is in surprise
That the stereo has ceased to pound.

A silence that pours and stirs
And settles down, brown inside my cup
And still is round about me,
When I drink it up.

Christine Curry, Brislington, Bristol, Avon

DUSK

The black is the black of night,
And the white is the white of day;
At their juxtaposition, their fusing
Their blending together,
Comes dusk.

A soft mellow time,
A calming stilly, space,
A time when the tired populace
Wends its weary way home.
When children settle to homework or TV.
In the gathering gloom, shadows creep onwards,
Wind rustles dry leaves,
Birds settle in well-woven nests.
Predators awake from daytime slumbers,
And prepare to forage for the night's pickings.

It's a time when the world itself
Stretches out its tired limbs,
Flexes its muscles, and relaxes;
It is at peace with itself;
It is the dusk.

Sarah Fernandes, Westbury-on-Trym, Bristol, Avon

THROWING SNOWBALLS AT THE MOON

Scarf-snug,
almost hesitant to trespass,
you trek paths, lushed with frost.
I slip, slide,
stride into your patterned steps.

Our laughter trickles through the hush;
coldness chafes cheeks,
blasts throats,
childhood tangs our tongues.

With burning fingers
we scoop up spheres of snow to pelt the moon,
aim again and again until darkness trembles,
branches spill ice crystals,
breath swirls in a dance of phantoms.

Dreams seep through darkened windows
of the night's last hours.
In amazing silence
we sink into a drift, lie star-still,
relive a myth of angels.

Margaret Holli, Warmley, Bristol, Avon

DON'T WANT

"Don't want bloody tea,"
Said she wearily
In fraught memory
Of the night he left.

"Don't want this damn pain
I'd be quite insane
To trust life again
When all men just lie."

The kindly male nurse
Excused every curse
For he'd witnessed worse
When binding her wrists.

She studied his face
Blushed sudden disgrace
Then started to trace
The curve of his smile.

The dawn ward glowed pink
Then struggling to think
She gave him a wink
And reached for her tea.

Ann Taylor, Trowbridge, Wiltshire

BOX HILL

I am
The glorious sweep of the hillside
On a hot June morning,
I am the dust that rises from the tinder track, now rough and
flying,
with the wheels of countless motorbikes
As they form a herd of wildebeest in the valley bottom.

I am
The smell of oil and rubber,
I am the sheen of polish and leather,
I am the heat and terror of a clan gathering
And the kiss of a small boy on his first ride,
For his grandfather.

Susan Harwood, Chippenham, Wiltshire

AND THIS DEEP, COLD BREATH IS ...

And this deep, cold breath is ...
An expression, a heartbeat, an extension
Of what we used to call love.
Sitting here with space in between us,
Yes, a vacuum of silence, and no pitiful excuse,
Neither one of us daring to speak a word,
Only a deep, cold breath each,
Rhythmic, alternate,
Trying not to meet eye to eye,
Uncomfortable, suddenly;
Alone together without our third.
Love is .. Late? Dead?
Lost
In the silent space
That hovers above the table
Like an eternity.

Jennifer Pickup, Westbury, Wiltshire

KISSING: NOTICE TO USERS

After some informal easy-drinking
of honey-beer and light wine
You turn,
Elegant, crisp pick of the bunch
paying particular attention to nose, ears, back of neck and
Lips
Lushest pasture
to kiss.
A delicate sharp taste at first
A mouth-ladling of curds
Sweet savoury sauce
with a hint of passion swirling fruit
Succulent steamy sponge
Panting to pressure.
Beware the valve
Lest it escape
To scald
Your delicate heart.

Susan Hart, Colerne, Wiltshire

East
Anglia

DETONATION

And sometimes;
Love explodes upon you with its gentle violence,
Casting reason and intellect to the four winds.
Sweeping away your shambling grey existence,
With a new and glittering reality,
Infinitely more wondrous.

David Horan, Hardwick, Cambridgeshire

AT LYMPSTONE

Time is estuarial
Beats out to the broad sea

Even as we linger
At the harbour edge
Behind the beached boats
The cliff's red elbow
The tide's ebb and flow
Are ours also

Until the eye
Drawn to discern beyond the middle distance
Sees with a start the village slipped away
The nets, the pockmarked mud
Left far behind

Ahead only
The horizon's level
The gulls' indifference

Rex Collinson, Cottenham, Cambridgeshire

HIGH CONSTELLATIONS

We step outside to smoke
in the back garden of your house;
it is April and the night is sudden cold like deep black water,
the stars and sharp moon cut us to pieces with their beauty.

Our figures are not diminished
beneath the sky's great dome,
for the high constellations exalt us
and the silent air,
as if a distant bell were struck,
rings all around us.

Tony Bowland, Ely, Cambridgeshire

GUM BOOT DANCE: TABLE MOUNTAIN

It is still on Table Mountain, no wind,
and the schoolchildren, in their yellow and black uniform,
practice part of a gumboot dance
to break up the heat of the morning with a rhythm.

Sweaty American tourists take photographs
of each other,
with each other,
to show each other when they get back home.

Cape Town lies below,
glassy in the sunlight.
A city in a paperweight
the ocean stuck against the shore.

James Woodhouse, Wymondham, Norfolk

YESTERDAY'S CHILD

I pause;
and the child in me escapes
to climb the wooden stile.
Into the meadow of yesterday
where lush green grass and
nature's flowers bathe in the sun,
and summer showers swell the stream.

I wait;
for the inner child
whose hours are spun
chasing the shadows.
And the rays of the sun
touch the gossamer shawl
woven twixt the branch
and the tumbling wall.

I walk;
barefoot to the wooden stile
then turn and pause
to gaze awhile.
So many memories to mow
from the harvest of seeds
that youth did sow.

Daphne Stone, Sprowston, Norwich, Norfolk

RESHAPE WHILST DAMP

Things that catch you in the quiet times,
stir up the past like old garage paint
from the back, pulled out, gloopy and stirred
with a sharp, splintered stick.
The way a laugh will bring to mind a lover's name,
butter-soft mouth and sandpaper cheeks
(all the tall men were the nicest to you)
and how a friendship can rot whilst your back's turned,
and can't be reclaimed despite best efforts.

Crunched, foetal on a bathroom's checked floor,
you cry and a phone continues to ring.
Or you watch a red moon rise, in a city
Fifteen hundred miles from everything you know.

People's lives are their stories, made all the more poignant
by the bitter recalls,
they hang like damp washing, with weight and in knots,
buckling the line. And the spin cycle always shreds your
best underwear.

Michelle Clingan, Hadleigh, Ipswich, Suffolk

INSTRUCTIONS FOR SETTING THE SKY ON FIRE

First take a sheet of glass.
Hold it firm or curve it slightly.
Dip your fingers into pure, dry pigment -
Crimson, lemon, Prussian blue.
Spiral them across the glare.
Pick a Japanese paintbrush
Fashioned with gold leaf at its tip.
Outline the shapes that jump at you
And stare.

Listen to an instrumental solo,
a storm of weeping wind.
Fix your glance ahead and concentrate
on silhouetted trees in mist,
ragged red illuminations
of cloud and hill,
a road with no end in sight.

Claire Hamilton, Lowestoft, Suffolk

WHAT CONSTABLE AND GAINSBOROUGH SAW

I gazed into a Suffolk sky at sunset.
A sinking, blood-red sun had brilliance still
To blind my eyes with brightness yet,
So beauty, unseen, could not my soul with wonder fill.

Blind I was to the warm brown earth,
Its gentle slopes with carpets of green,
Which nurtures its sons, matures them from birth,
And lends them its character, rich but serene.

Likewise my love has a beauty so intense
That I in her presence again am blind.
Her loveliness and gentleness, only in her absence,
Can I clearly appreciate and call to my mind.

My vision has clarity now you have left me,
- But darling, come back, for I long not to see!

Raymond Hume, Sudbury, Suffolk

East
Midlands

WRITER'S BLOCK

The public are dissatisfied;
"Off with her head!"
I pick up the pen
and my mental block is black,
covered with velvet so as not to splinter
delicate white wrist.
Lay my papers upon the wood,
and I shall write my own obituary
(a sacrifice, a sonnet ...)
lay my head alongside the pages
on my velvet covered writer's block.
Axeman comes, in hood of silver
Stoops, then metaphorically,
(but oh so swiftly)
Cuts off my head.

Christy Allan, Alfreton, Derbyshire

ABSENCE

Your absence is like a desert,
A hot wind blowing through
The empty spaces where once
Thoughts jostled each other
In an attempt to reach perfection.
Now there is nothing
No spark of what was once there
Has been and then vanished,
Like the ever-moving air.

I see the pale yellow rocks
The red misty-ness of distance
Purpling into sky
Too hot to look at.
Each rock is a day,
Barren and lifeless
Angles jagged, crevices within,
Holding onto nothing.
Sand-covered footprints show
That I have been a prisoner here,
Until you came again.

Malise McGuire, Sinfin, Derby, Derbyshire

TOMORROW

Tomorrow.
Tomorrow, I said.
Did you not hear me?
Tomorrow I will be a good wife, a tolerant mother.
I won't shout -
I shouldn't shout; yes sometimes it's deserved
But often - not.
Just my frustration, may erupt and burn you.
Tomorrow, I said.
Tomorrow I will have time, make time.
Tomorrow I will pray more, smile more, grouch less.
Tomorrow I will feel like making love, may even instigate
the process ...
Tomorrow, I said.
Tomorrow I will not feel guilty
About my imperfect home, imperfect family,
Imperfect self ...
But then, tomorrow we will all be better,
More secure, more happy,
Less analytical.
What a difference a day can make.

Julia Westhead, New Mills, Derbyshire

PERMANENT

At first meeting I smelt fixative
In your clothes and hair
Precious things: let none fade nor flounder

You paraded permanent words
Whilst I struggled to remember whether waves
Were permanent

Or was it matter not movement that remained
I had decided to leave with my confusion when
To prove your point

You strapped tap shoes to your feet
What I can do with these abides
You said but when I stop the dance will cease

And so I stayed
And now we both switch on and off
the dance hall lights

K M Abel, Wormhill, Derbyshire

REGENERATION

Her grandmother, she said, handing me
the photo I was supposed to restore,
its corners worn, dog-eared, coated
by layers of Irish mist and the imprints
of generations of admiring thumbs.
She'd been a young girl then.

She's turned away from the prying lens,
looking out perhaps over moorland
or at young men lifting crates of cod,
or musing on unborn children, unaware
of this crease that will furrow her brow
and the blemish that could pass for a blush.

I do as required, shading in, burning out,
judge the exact exposure, determine
the moment to fix emerging features.
The likeness takes shape in the cradling tray,
imperfections purged, the miasma removed,
reborn at last, a lifeless resurrection.

Alan Anthony, Quarndon, Derbyshire

MIRRORS

In a maze of inward facing mirrors
all I see is myself.
Different mirrors show me my
different gifts.
Some stretched and thin,
Others small, weak and vulnerable.
But when I wander into the last mirror.
It shows me with God and I am perfect.
God makes us perfect however much my different skills
vary in strength.
God builds up your own custom person.
You.

Matt Green, Loughborough, Leicestershire

IN THE PARK

Walking through the park today
Poems fluttered from the trees
Alighting on my hair and clothes,
Murmuring in the salad-scented air.
Sentences sprang out of the ground,
Snaking across the grass,
While words buzzed and hummed in the flowerbeds,
As the sky endlessly rechalked itself in soft smudges,
Its fleecy flotillas tugging at our spirit strings.
And if only I'd had the time ...
What a work of art I'd have written!
But two-and-a-half years of fearless girl,
Commandeered the chronic chronicler in me,
And played and played out her own masterpiece,
Running and climbing, swinging and swooping,
Ladling out her laughter with cups of pretend tea,
Her eyes beaming with heaven.
And afterwards, she slept all the way home.

Una Bentley, Market Harborough, Leicestershire

THAT HOUSE

That house! No I'll never forget that house
the east wind blew straight through
and dark hills brooded close;

the wind gathered up the fire
danced it across the moon
reflecting blood-red shadows into the room

cold as a long dead forge;
and the sea seeped into the sun
salt shapes edging into dark corners

while the east wind keened like mourners
rat-tatting frames as a drum
as mist slithered the cracks

and yews bent their backs
to a moon dressed as a ghost.
That house! No, I'll never forget that house

Bette Walklate, Leicester, Leicestershire

PERFECTION

The gardeners of suburbia
Sip afternoon tea
On manicured lawns
Where no weed dare be.

Perfect clipped hedges
Stand tall and straight
Roses are trained
Over the garden gate.

Beds of annuals
In strict formation
Are planted with
Military regulation.

But give me a hedgerow
In England in May
With fresh green hawthorn
That's lost its way.

Soft arching blossom
Lacy, delicate and sweet
Ever will make
My heart miss a beat.

Susan Barker, Gainsborough, Lincolnshire

NINE NAILS

I thought you the most beautiful boy I had ever seen.
To know you, intimately. Your slim thighs; springs of hair
You would wrap around your fingers, once, twice, three times.
Your brown eyes, stirred melted chocolate, were made for
Licking my lips. The black-bathed, Brecon mountains no more
                                                    wonderful.
Five young rivers rush in one, maelstromic mass. Six o'clock
We agree to meet and follow the Severn to the nipple sucking
                                                        sea.
We drove the length of our land. Watching whatever you ate,
                                              you
Ravenous and quickly satisfied. Is it nine nails that a coffin
                                                    takes?

Stephanie Tillotson, Boston, Lincolnshire

THREADS

I wake at dawn to face another day
Designed for toil, designed for tedium,
Whose sameness ever grows more wearisome
My body finds it harder to obey
For youth's vitality has slipped away,
My head is filled with pandemonium
Which reels and spins until I'm overcome;
The fabric of my life's in disarray.

But each new day another thread bestows,
Mixed hues to work into life's tapestry;
And though the duller shades portend our woes,
Within the threads of that embroidery,
Among the richest of them all are those
That brought you and your constant love to me.

Hilary Cairns, Retford, Nottinghamshire

ANNOTATION FOR A POEM THAT WAS NEVER WRITTEN

The opening lines sweeping across the page
like the hills outside of his window.
Gaps filled with the rolling colour of sky, of corn, of sea
light the narrative elements of the verse.
His view translated into the hearts and minds of his readers.

Then as the central theme draws you in, harsh, almost
demonic
reflecting his circumstance, the death of his wife, his lover.
No more the bright sky, the golden corn, the blue sea.
Dark the page becomes saddening the verse.
His soul bared to the hearts and minds of his readers.

The finale, the lines growing across the paper
like the sweep of an artist's brush, his hobby, art, life,
bring back hope, banish the cloud, harvest the corn, tame the
sea,
shade the construction of the words in the verse.
His spirits strength melded into the hearts and minds of his
readers.

Martin Spooner, Worksop, Nottinghamshire

LOST SOULS

The hulls of souls;
Gutted by the sharpness of life's knife,
Their insides scraped and scoured,
Left scarred and inflamed like a lung freed of its cancer;
Lie, decaying ruins at the bottom of unfed hearts,
The wreckage barely visible through the dank mists
And cloudy waters the world has injected there.

Their venomous vapours
Choke the passion and innocence of youth
And fog the path of pure love.
Ambition is squashed under the weight of the ruin,
Hope and happiness lie there too,
Too stifled and suffocated to raise a breath or call out.

Drowning and dying,
The lost souls flounder and clasp, to gasp their last.
The bodies which house them lose colour and life,
Begin to fade and fail
And are crushed beneath the weight of failure.
The world looks on accusingly,
Not thinking to blame itself.

Stephan Richeux, Edwinstowe, Mansfield, Nottinghamshire

SLOW RELEASE

She left him
slowly

by small degrees

each by itself
too small
to notice

made quiet withdrawals
from their joint
account

turned down
the volume

dimmed
the lights

Something's changed,
he thought

just can't put
my finger
on it

Chris Ridge, Silverstone, Northamptonshire

AUGUST GRASSES

Under the sun
the grass has grown golden.
Swaying in the blue
where once it was green
with high-hopping insects
flying, with all
the world's busy traffic.
Pirates of pollen
raiding richly-laden larders;
making the sky noisy
by their trading.
Chirping and humming
and grasses growing
until, under the sun
they come
to a quiet time
of firm and golden
nakedness
in a blue space
with harvest's wind whispering.

Jim Trevorrow, Corby, Northamptonshire

GOING BACK

She fills my day with tides of despair
When she yearns to go back
Back to Nottingham, the Trent, to him.
Can she not see the majesty of this?
Where tufts of grass fringed white on dune
Sprout like whiskers on an old man's beard.
Hoary, dishevelled.
Can she not see the splendour of this?
When a solitary tern circles high overhead
And a stray dog roots in pockets of whispering sand.
Can she not see the freedom of this?
When mature students frolic along shore
Scuffing sand like overgrown teenagers
Or feel the lap of water over feet
Or see Portmadoc shimmering across the bay.
I think not.

Monica Norgate, Oakham, Rutiand

West Midlands

FUTURISM ART EXHIBITION

All those violet triangles
And school uniform green rectangles,
The dead mechanical
Compositions
Of red parrots, yellow waves
Hollow faces, of
Bayonets in the brain
- Or were they machine guns
(The forward-moves of the Hun).

There was an absence of roses blooming,
Smell of early morning dews,
Of long-distance horizons
In the sunlight,
Of nights and crickets and barbecues.
The tropical island was
A map of curlycues
Flattened, dissected,
Its guts, a perfectly formed snail
In peuce and ice blue

I do like the museum's cafeteria though.

Penelope Hart, Hereford, Herefordshire

SHREWSBURY

The floods return. The town stands in lake -
Fields of water. The through-flowing
Severn sweeps broader,
Deeper. Willows are half-under.
Swans swim up to front doors
Half-real, half fairy-tale.
People stand; take in the new angle,
A car park of metal roofs in a reservoir

Unwelcome; yet here is a glitter of freedom;
As it swells under Greyfriars Bridge
Look to this rushing water
Now bearing the weight of light
As the wild sun spills its brilliance
Like a pot of paint. Racing past us
Ferocious as lava
The river charges full spate -
A torrent of horses - a thunder of silver.

Caroline Ackroyd, Shrewsbury, Shropshire

RELEASE

To feel normal again
Was such a relief. Release from the night watch
From staring at shadows on a playground floor
Clarity made me real
How ill I had been
Talking to unwashed plates
(It's not me, doctor, it's my daughter, she thinks she's God)

I was terrified by the loss
You can't replace time in pill form
So I let them go
And looked for old friends
Amongst pens and pencils
Tools of diagnosis

Nick Lawrence, Tamworth, Staffordshire

SLEEPING BEAUTY WAKES

Rising through drifts of slow dreams - of bees
in lavender, voices half known, an arrow's plumed flight -
I sense seasons changing. Sunlight shifts
over flagged floor, a sour greenness turns russet.
Sometimes a dead branch cracks, there's tearing
of ivy ripped from stone, a panting scuffle that brings
a moist hand fumbling to my neck, stale breath
hot on my cheek. I freeze, still as death.

Once in some far-off land they made me
learn to curtsy, sing courtly airs, recite and sew
straight seams to Nurse's nagging. Now let me be.
Swaddled in fur coverlets, I'm free to summon
a troubadour's shy smile, velvet at my breast, juice of warm
plums,
to float, light as swansdown, through unknown doorways.

Amanda Parkyn, Penkridge, Staffordshire

I MISS YOU

I miss you.
Not with that heart constricting anguish
of loss and loneliness
when plural becomes singular, because
we were not a couple, just a pair.
I miss you in trivialities,
in little griefs that pepper my day.
The phone rings and I expect
your weary "Hello", which
you always said two-tone.
And when I can't identify a plant,
or need a compassionate ear,
a tolerant soul, a back-up crew,
I miss you.
Fate dealt us unfair hands, held separately
but giving us the rapport of shared experience
that cannot be replaced.
You left me the sole keeper
of our childhood.
And I miss you.

Elspeth Malloch, Lichfield, Staffordshire

REFLECTION

The seventh arc in water colours.
The aunt I barely knew.
Paints with hues of blues,
Once splashed cheerful blooms of spring.

The lane we walked together,
Now drained of rainbow colour -
Mystery, magic, dreams
No more invoked.

Violet fades ...
To leave regret.

Catherine Roth, Burton-upon-Trent, Staffordshire

MATINEE

Face the audience,
Take a bow.
For it is a performance, you and I.

Behind the scenes;
The puppet master,
Pulling the strings.
We'll be back after this short commercial break.

...Centre stage.
Let's pretend
This isn't a Greek tragedy.
Instead,
A happy ever after.
Let's pretend.

Encore,
Encore.

Dawn Vince, Rugby, Warwickshire

A BROTHER'S RECOLLECTION

With my sister and mother,
Stories around the open fire.
Tub of butter at the ready,
Bread toasted on the flames
With an unbelievably long fork.

Shadows dance on the ceiling
As tales of old Ireland
Fill the unlit room.
Green, white and gold
Tainted by black and tan.

Another piece of toast,
Hot cocoa burns my tongue
And froths my lip.
"Off to bed you two,
school in the morning."

At some unearthly hour
I hear the sound of key
Turning in front door.
Dad returns from his night shift.
I drift back to sleep.

Tony Elmore, Shard End, Birmingham, West Midlands

A THANK YOU SKY

I open the window to a thank you sky,
to a sliver of moon, to the distant smog
of a dying sunset, a spectrum blurring to the land's edge
where the air is a smudged and foggy lilac.

So I find the evening's artwork here where you've hung it.
So I summon them and they come with cameras
to record the embers, the trees dipped
in layers of mist, like swathed waders,

and the village lamps, regular and hazy.
Then the moon bows, horizons dim and darken,
and having savoured, shared, I leave them there,
tasting; my photograph is a pen and paper.

Nathan Hawkins, Coventry, West Midlands

SADNESS

There is sadness in the world tonight
Falling in the raindrops
Singing its way into our ears
It touches us
Penetrates all
Tonight

Seeping through the cracks in our dreams
Sleep failing to protect its charges
Soaking through our floors
And climbing up our spines
Sadness colours us all tonight

Tonight, sadness enters our homes and our souls
Brushing the shoulders of the world as it passes

Gina Roberts, Quinton, Birmingham, West Midlands

ANNA

Do not let them say that your hair is brown.
It is auburn and golden, copper and chestnut,
As ambers of autumn shine bronze in the sunlight.

Do not let them say that your eyes are blue.
They are sapphire and azure and summer skies,
The colour of eggshells and clear cool seas.

Do not let them say that your skin is white.
It is china and rose petal, all pearl and pinks,
The colour of shells with the blossoms of spring.

Kate Diaram, Walsall, West Midlands

FOURTH DIMENSION

Stubborn clocks relentlessly tick,
Ignorant of the future, careless of the past -
Stuck in the quality of nowness,
Fearlessly mincing forward,
Perceiving nothing.

Another swing, another tock,
Marking time like an infinity of zeros -
So sit too, the lives of the mortal.

In another place free spirits soar,
Oblivious,
Weaving their signals through space,
Ignorant of the meaning of tick
Or tock.
Knowing what they should not know
Before the clock's time is due,
Courtesy of the fourth dimension.

Angus McLeod, Worcester, Worcestershire

LEAVES ME SILENT

We watched the moon, my son and I,
A quiet and gentle sharing of the night sky,
Waiting for the night-blind sun to hide
The tranquil sea and turn its silver tide
To an eclipsed ebony of red and gold.
And in that shared moment of history, I told
Him, "You will remember this." "Even when I'm old?"
"Oh yes, even then." "You too?" "Oh yes, me too."

How strange that far-off face of age
Which for him is beyond the nearness of space or sage.
Yet even as I watch he changes, ever
Moving into a maturity beyond the baby I bore.
He must find the depth of a countless forever
And find his place within its core.

While my love for him, my man-child,
As constant as the moon is mild,
Enfolds and cradles him as
The galaxy cradles star dust:
And fills me with a wonder which just
Leaves me silent.

Carey Jane Hardy, Redditch, Worcestershire

North West

FAITH

I'm poised high on a rocky outcrop crag
between the rolling boiling molten land
and stony frozen sea
I take a burning breath of poisoned air
and lift my arms
imagine wings
and leap

Genevieve Harding, Northwich, Cheshire

THE DANCE OF THE WHITE BUTTERFLIES

The warmth of the sun on my back,
dandelion seeds floating contentedly,
caressing and tingling
as they land on bare skin.

White butterflies dancing,
teasing
longing for more.
A deep urging inside me.

Surrounded by pinks and lilacs of petals
and the light trickling
of water nearby.
The butterflies rest

and nestle together,
lightly fluttering.
I lie with you,
nothing else matters.

Lucy Roberts, Crewe, Cheshire

BOYCHILD

the grass is a whirlpool, he said
he ran and sang and the elongated
glass rain spat up the world's dry dust
spat up my feet and the stark trees purred
the muttering moths, still, in tearful quiet
and the grass was so green, the whirlpool grass
the shadows soaking through the soil

no-one can pass through my shield of fire he said

Jennifer Adams, Bredbury, Stockport, Cheshire

THE MAN OF YESTERDAY

Slowly snaked the storm by day,
creeping, clothed in deceit of way.
Darkness hiding the true enormity,
until a flash of lightning pain, caused deathly threat -
deformity.

Clutching heart with hand of fear,
is the reaper coming here?
Groaning, twisting roars the thunder,
down and down he goes - asunder.

Numbness now with blind hysteria
leaves him there, now inferior.
Still and muzzled, prostrate lay,
the man of yesterday.

Barbara Edmondson, Warrington, Cheshire

LENNOX WOOD

Skin, smooth and flattened by time,
As if oak branches laid shadows upon his brow.
Mouth laden with passages of silence
Lips glistening like shards of pale, pink ice.
Heaviness clings to him like grime
Days surrounded by sleep.
Eyes full of memories that rise, as vapour,
Through the cobwebbed surfaces of the mind
A voice turned to rust by the years
And by nights of hard drinking.
Lost in a half-world of darkness
With a scent of dust and mould
And deep, sour bitterness.
Meaningless thoughts, scattered
As wind-whipped ashes.
Someone worshipped him once.
He has glorified her beyond truth
In a fragmented history
Of his youth.
Touched by his sadness
I leave him to believe.

Lesley Conquest, Chester, Cheshire

MOONY NIGHT

I sipped each breath straight from the moony sky.
My face lay bathed in coolness like the night.
One instant's opening of my sleep-mused eyes
Disclosed the moon all hazed about with space.
Each heartbeat pulsing in my ears proclaimed me part of
this,
And made me smile in sleep. The morning made me sigh
To accept the severance of life from Life was hard.
And then, my daughter came with morning tea
And in it, mirrored bright but very small, the moon!
I swallowed it and smiled.

J Buckley, Penrith, Cumbria

THE GARDEN OF IMAGININGS

In the garden of imaginings, I'll take a walk with you.
But you must close your eyes, or you might obscure the
view.
Breathe deep the heady scents of the flowers as they blend,
Then kiss the rose again and the dream will never end.

I feel the gentle stirrings of the fingers of a breeze.
I hear the whispering voices of the breath among the trees.
I taste the honey nectar of the kisses of the sun,
Vision blurred by branches as they mingle into one.

The supple grass caresses me, beneath me, and inside
The confines of my garden nothing needs to hide.
In the garden of imaginings I'll give you dreams to share,
But you must close your eyes. If you wake, I won't be there.

Tracey Turner, Barrow-in-Furness, Cumbria

129

TIME, SPACE, AND ALL THAT STUFF

Nothing is there. We balance in it
Like fish buoyed up by miles of water.
We cannot touch the hours and the minutes
Or hear the sound of before and after.

It is nobody's fault. No-one began it,
Wound up the clock or signed a paper.
There was no plan for the global caper,
No bastard decided to drop us in it.

No candle-flame or prayer-wheel's spinning,
Muezzin's chant or bardic keening,
No zealot's sums or druggy dreaming
Can make an end or start a beginning.

We cannot fix it, we may not make it.
The sequence set before we began, it
Comes with terms we cannot break, it
Would be like this, whatever the planet.

The ocean is dark, and what comes after
Drowning is darker. Stars are glowing.
Slowly the knowable yields to our knowing,
Slowly the fish get used to the water.

David Craig, Carnforth, Cumbria

A DYING FALL

September is eating into summer,
her teeth-marks clear in the sharpening air
and thinning light. Against this bleaching sky,
trees reveal their full extent of beauty
when, summoned by love, tired leaves rehearse
a parting song with the breeze, more awake
now that they may soon sleep, more deeply green
to point the imminence of autumn's gold.

Poised on the brink, September trees exude
that surrender which is exhaustion's gift:
the leaves will soon cease to breathe and, flaming,
will die then, and drop, ushered on their way
by wind; not untouched by melancholy,
yet acquiescing still in the movement
of the real - the flooding through bright bold death
to mercy, to rest, on the waiting earth.

Lucy Crispin, Kendal, Cumbria

GOODBYE

Think of me as a flower,
Budded and soaked in dew.
Remember our friendship,
When it was fresh and new.

Think of me as a butterfly,
On a sunny summer's day.
That fluttered into your life,
And then just flew away.

Think of me as green leafy trees,
Coloured by time and wafted away in the autumn breeze.
Think of me as a snowy winter's day,
A moment frozen in time that really could not stay.

Friendship in seasons,
Always moving on my friend.
And as they say,
All good things must come to an end.

And friendship also changes,
This we can see.
But as the seasons change,
My friend - think of me.

Susan Richardson, Longtown, Carlisle, Cumbria

SLOW BURN

I turn the poker twice then push
the end into the green-birch bark.
Heat draws out the rain in a hiss of mist.

I am silenced but not still, racing
around forests of history, scavenging
for crumbs to trace your path back to mine,

seeking to bring back the wasted time,
seasoned and carved to fit our stiffened lives.
We missed the moment when silence drifted

from golden to red, dyed in regret.
The words cracked around us
like the elm, brittle with disease.

I turn the poker once more, draw it out
and with its heated tip, brand our initials
into the young wood - a mark to say

once we were here, and we loved.

Vik Bennett, Windermere, Cumbria

I STILL GET A THRILL

I still get a thrill
at seeing that swatch of doorkey grey sea
when I look westward between buildings by the prom.
Some days it looks as cold and blank
as a bull's eye in a butcher's dustbin;
put your feet in its flatness
and the ankles would be chopped through
like bacon on a slicer.
Other days, the sun seeps through the clouds
and tinsels the tips of the waves
like a spilt box of staples.
On rare days, the sun is pinned
like a Lib-Dem rosette in a Tory sky
and everyone votes to go paddling.

Lyn Punt, Blackpool, Lancashire

TEMPUS

Sitting alone in a brightly lit café.
Clawed hands clutching the warming cup.
Misty eyes gaze through Arabica perfume.
People pass by, and she never looks up.

What does she see in the ribbons of steam?
Who does she hear in the voice of the crowds?
Where does she go as she sits all alone?
Back to the time when she stood tall and proud?

As memories pass the window one by one.
The younger she smiles out from her old lips.
She used to be a goddess on the dancefloor.
There's no more dancing on arthritic hips.

You can't wish back time, it goes too fast.
Dance as hard as you like, you can never catch up.
Time stirs you around. You're there, then you're gone.
She watches the bubbles in her cold coffee cup.

Gillian Constable, Accrington, Lancashire

ANGRY WATER

The water pent within narrow confines
roars and rages, tumbles, threatening relentless
a continuous powerful teeming torrent
Carrying us where we would not venture
Crushing us in anger against soiled unyielding rock.
Crushing us again and again, consumed force, fear, frus-
tration, foaming and bubbling ever downward.
Dragging all who come into contact down, down, down.
Ravenous, revengeful, railing, roaring, racing.

Downstream, a different scene; very different yet the same,
in truth, can it be the same river?
So calm and still, deep and tranquil, quiet.
Mirroring the sentinel trees on its green banks
Pale blue sky, in the fading light, reflected.
What makes the difference?
No longer confined within itself, it found expression, relief
in overflowing.
Its late state more peaceable by contrast,
than if the anger had never been.
Sharing, refreshing, loving and being loved.

Joy Wheatcroft, Brierfield, Lancashire

PORTENT

Zephyrus sends an almighty gust,
agile wings direct its thrust,
black crows ride the sky
then rest on branches high,
jet beaks rattle and scold
turning warriors' blood stone cold.

Horny tools with precision pierce,
exposed old flesh once fierce,
jet beaks rattle and scold,
amongst carrion their work unfolds.

Dominic Cooper, Burnley, Lancashire

CRASH TEST DUMMY

After all these years,
I've finally worked out
What it is that I am;
I'm an experiment
In human endurance;
How much can the species take
Before it breaks up?
And when I'm mashed up;
Smashed against a laboratory wall,
Broken beyond all repair,
There's always more
To take my place.
As I feel big, rough hands
Strapping me into the seat of death,
I can hear my maker's laughter -
"You're a crash test, Dummy."

Andy Chadwick, Preston, Lancashire

THE ACCIDENT

I don't remember anything
Of the accident except waking up
By the concrete bus shelter,
Then shutting the door of the dented car.

Being guided into the old woman's house,
Dripping, bloodstaining the carpet,
Sitting by the bathroom sink, screaming,
A front tooth missing, nose sideways.

Then, enter the wailing ambulance,
I am placed in a chair and pushed
In the back, neckbraced,
And driven to the hospital.

Dripping. Swabs! Scalpel! Surgical
Instrumentation! A horror of bone,
Tissue and swells, a twisted wreckage
Greeting guests (sobbing uncontrollably)

Louder than my painkilled, morphined self
Laying there motionless, emotionless
On a bed of nylon nails, empty.

Scott Mallett, Fleetwood, Lancashire

EARTHWATCH

Time passed in a golden haze
Leaving a panorama of memories
Drifting down the river,
With the soft whispering summer breeze
Browsing in the bushes -
And a stir of light in the willows
Like the flashing of a thousand
Silver minnows.
Then came the wild streams of
Violet midnight,
Vortices glittering with dust of gold
In those wide ultimate spaces.
And she was part of the mystery
And beauty of it all,
Earth in her mantle
With those dark, dream-haunted skies
Descending.

Peter Rigby, Clitheroe, Lancashire

INVISIBLE

Like a scene from a film, in fuzzy monochrome,
he sits by the window, but no-one sees.

Grey hair, grey suit, stiff collar and tie,
he's going out, but no-one knows,
and he eats alone, crumbly bread,
and a bit of tasty cheese.
A crumb sticks to his lip, but no-one sees.

He's going out, but there's no-one
to say goodbye to an old man,
frail as a dry twig, carrying
cake and a flask,
carefully wrapped like treasure.

In the hospital, a regular visitor,
no-one notices this bearer of cake,
and love, sitting quietly,
holding the hand of his wife
whose mind has floated away.

Invisible, unrecognised he shares his cake,
and no-one notices him leave.

Eileen Hudson, Rochdale, Greater Manchester

THE LONGEST DAY

Twelve after sunrise
Six before sunset
You breathed your first
In that chromed room
Of tubes
And dangerous-looking instruments

Eighteen of light that day
An eyeful of dark the rest
And you in the middle
Solstice child
Meeting your dark father
Dry as the desert
Your fair mother
Weeping rain

Light years apart
Dark minutes passing
And you in-between with nothing
But your life
Pulsing in their hearts
On that unequal day

Phil McNally, Bolton, Greater Manchester

COMPANY

From pubs he brings them;
One by one to his flat in the suburbs,
Offering drinks in neat glasses,
Conversation spanning the public and private eye
And music he stylishly explains.

Life, they think, isn't so bad after hours;
The laughter and chatter,
Head thrown back in a pleasing mix.

From nowhere, from behind,
With an old school tie;
Quickly, tightly, longer, longing,
Finally letting go, to slump in the chair.

Sitting them upright,
Straightening their hair and cushions,
Refreshing glasses,
And signalling a new toast,
They spend the night,
Bringing in the dawn.

Len Evans, Fallowfield, Greater Manchester

AGEING

When passion wrinkles with increasing age,
What will take its sweating place?
When the stuffing has less thyme than sage,
What luring smile will sweep the varicose face?

If fleshless hands grope without hope
And winking eye winks all the time,
When bony limbs can no longer cope,
Heights of ecstasy no longer climb,
What in place will lovers find,
A love not of body but of mind?

But if old brains decay and are fermented,
If minds not clear become demented,
What will become of love once so sure?
Will souls love forevermore?

David Ryder, Middleton, Greater Manchester

IMAGINATION

I have seen where the sunlight starts.
High above the mountain,
where the air is clear.
The sun is golden and
the raindrops ride on the wings of the birds.

I have heard the water with
its fierce avenging roar,
chase the fleeing rocks down the river bed.
Where the ground is hard and
the earth is thirsty.

I have flown with the wind
through the great forests.
Where the trees bow in deference.
Tenderly borne, my own invention.
I am imagination and your brainchild
Your mind's third eye. I am Spirit
And I never die.

Jean Lees, Irlam, Greater Manchester

SPEAK MY NAME SOFTLY

Speak my name softly when our love has ceased to be
and coldness twists around your heart,
If bitterness lies in your words then say the least you can,
That you may learn to live apart
from me.

Speak my name kindly when you are gone and free
and new love perhaps to you has come,
Yet in forgetting all your pain, you have forgotten me,
In silence then I as deaf and dumb
shall be.

June Knight-Boulton, Newton-le-Willows, Merseyside

THE POSE

I saw a portrait of a small, still girl,
Centuries old, her powdered head a-curl,
Her hands clasping her cat - a pampered pet,
Her pose unchildlike, her expression set.
Pressed into formal shape, in stiff brocade,
What weary hours had passed as paint was laid
Beautifully on the canvas as she sat
Longing for sunlit freedom with her cat?

Did she, released, tear off the tight blue dress?
In comfortable robe, freed from the corset's stress,
Flee down the hall with loosened, sunny curls
to play, maybe, with other little girls?

J Offord, Southport, Merseyside

THE WOMAN DOWNSTAIRS

Tonight the relentless birds call for hours and hours,
Fooling me into thoughts of springtime and light ...
Of nights spent camping out in the park and lazy April
afternoons
Composing sonnets for all the -
The fullness of the mid-February moon
Combines with the thin net curtains to create a mesh effect
on the bed -
Trapping me in a web of frittered lemonade light.

Such things don't distract me.
They merely increase the tension and the wretched, longing
feeling in my gut.
It's the woman in the downstairs flat who captures my
mind
And every single glimmer of thought within it.

Some nights her whispered weeping haunts me.
At other times the gentle sound of her soft Scottish accent
Lulls me out of concentration, as she talks
To her geraniums, her magnolias
And her dying mother on the phone.

I stand and stare at the ticking of the clock.

Daniel Smith, Higher Bebington, Merseyside

COME FOR A RIDE

She was unpegging her washing in the garden one eve
When the sun started flirting through the fluttering trees.
"Come for a ride," he said.

Hands on hips she turned. "What! With three kids to entertain,
And my eldest at war in the Gulf? You've no shame!"

The sun showered her with light - diamond and gold
And caressed her in a warm, honey glow.

"Come on," he urged "for the ultimate ride.
Can't you see your children all well occupied?"

She stretched up slowly to meet his warm kiss
And all her stone-heavy thoughts were whisked
Into a frivolity of cirrus, where she rose.
Like a bubble over rooftops and higher until
all became a mosaic of earthenware, blue and green.

She smiled in devotion to spinning around
The burning essence that her lover bestowed
Until she slipped softly, by the degree,
into the darkening air.
"Goodnight," said he.

Catherine Waud, Formby, Merseyside

THE POET

"I'll write you a poem," she said
As if it were
A gift, a joy to do it
To cut deep into the secret passions
And let the blood of fear and pain run free

To catch the words
That scorch like formless maniacs
Through the labyrinthine echoes
of the mind

To force a shape
Upon the wisps and shadows of a memory
That hovers, then flees
Beyond the hound of comprehension

To conjure up a world
From fragments of some karmic field
Long dead or still to come

"I'll write you a poem," she said

Patricia Fleming, Liverpool, Merseyside

North
East

149

AN INTREPID CORRELATION

How the land rises and falls and the river
Meanders across the fertile industrialised plain.
Try to comprehend the geography
Just two minutes walk from the bus station
The road leaves from London, here I strayed
Frightened by the shade although meekly mixing
With the local carnivores, new-born and knowing nothing.
Earlier years in Amsterdam, repeating stories
In a claustrophobic house of beaten
Complex characters under lowering skies.
The night we danced is the night that exists
Numinous and born of beauty and fear.
As the wind strengthens in the graveyard
And dark clouds begin to hover
Attendant ghosts animate the landscape
And the dinosaur cries of gulls blend with sirens.
But I sleep in a fog, blinkered with sagging skin
Recalling sudden careless moves to her
Unthinking and unredeemed, I lack the heroic gesture.

Richard Pink, Middlesbrough, Cleveland

TRUE LOVE

You remind me that I claim
betrayal as my style
and I stumble at the truth.

But, like my mentor
I reply by smiling
"Who loves you more than I?"

Ed Turley, Wolsingham, County Durham

A RECIPE FOR A BRUISED EGO

A little patience wrapped in a smile,
A kiss, a cuddle, engineered with guile.
Add a pinch of gentle persuasion,
Strong hands to caress and ease consternation.
A twist of flattery, not too contrived
And a tissue, to wipe tears from the eyes.
Just a whisper, no more in condemnation,
Much more is achieved in quiet contemplation.
Fold in a mixture of love and of trust,
Then let simmer a while, that is a must.
Apply freely with kindness and genuine emotion
When massaging the ego with this potent potion.

Cyril Matthews, Newton Aycliffe, County Durham

POEM FOR A DEAD LOVER

I can still feel your arms around me
I still see your shadow on the wall
Your smile still haunts my dreams
Your laugh echoes in my mind.

Abandonment hovers over my head
Endless rain floods my heart
But I'm still holding on to you
I cannot ever let you go
Because if I say goodbye
Then you're gone forever
And everything will crumble away.

I hear your voice
Echoing round the house
We once shared.
I look for you
Search every room
In the dead of night
In the darkest hour.
All I find are painful reminders
That you will never come home.

Catherine Burgin, Darlington, County Durham

THE ANGEL OF THE NORTH

We've got an angel in our yard.
Gran says, "No 'cos an angel sings,
All angels have pretty faces,
Halos and feathers in their wings.

Angels are made by God," Gran says,
Then she pretends to cough 'cos she
Doesn't have any idea
What angels really might be.

Not made of bolts, steel and copper
With wings shaped like huge lolly sticks,
Two hundred tons or so it weighs,
Never fly, drop like loads of bricks.

Will it stand being twisted in
Winds of hundred miles for hours?
"Better had," says Dad and Tommy,
"This 'ere angel is all ours!"

Myra Bowen, Hexham, Northumberland

SWEET TEXT

Slow talk.
Talk in slow motion
Through the treacle of the sky.
Sweet words gently stirred with tender thoughts.
Feelings and emotions crystallised and carefully arranged.
Finger wrapped into electronic parcels,
For your tongue to taste and fondle,
To share the flavour of love.
Passion toffees, tender sherbet touches,
Crunchy nougat hugs, the kiss of chocolate.
Pleasures, once shared, now shared again,
The past made present, memories preserved.
This electronic blender of letters awaits its ingredients.
I have them all - all, that is, but you.

Owen Sutherland, Hepscott, Morpeth, Northumberland

SHADOWS

A shadow as dark and uncompromising as the deepest
depths of pandemonium crept upon the black and white
portrait of your paper lungs, forming a rock of hard lead in
your ever-gasping throat.

Poison as lethal as the apple that tempted Eve, violently
thrashed through your ageing veins and stole the bubbling
twinkle from your once so vibrant eyes.

The angels shining in white that surrounded your heavy
bed, tried so hard, but they just couldn't help to keep you
alive.

Marissa Carruthers, Newcastle, Tyne and Wear

ALONE

The flow of the moon is folding
Your blood turns to oil and starts twisting

Voices stagger from pallid lips
Deep yellow field surrounds
And drowns

Flat grey skies reflect the patience in your eyes
But that boy's are blue
And unhindered

Insects chirrup
Disturbed
Near the church

Applying lipstick
And preparing hands

Wets leaves on board
Smuggled under shoes
Tasting new bought soles

And so must you start at first like those

Untied
Broke
Alone

Graeme Beech, Sunderland, Tyne and Wear

CYCLE

New green, bursting fresh reflecting pale.
Deepening green, vibrant young and lasting green.
Warmer green and golden, blue and pink and yellow.
Beautiful kaleidoscope on green and gold.

Ageing slowly to red and brown, drifting, gently falling
down.
Swishing brown carpet, gone is the glow.
Grey above stark black pointing fingers.
Wet shining dark brown below.

Drier and harder, lighter in colour,
Here and there edged in bleak white.
Harder and bleaker, dull sameness surrounding,
Then whiteness and whiter and whiteness again.
A glory of whiteness a smooth curved soft whiteness,
Lying in wait for the green.

Cyril Dick, Hull, East Yorkshire

HOLY ISLAND

Without you tonight I roam
The footprints of your love for me
Retrace our steps and stand upon the place
Where once we knew
Whatever would befall we two
Would be a fall from grace as when
We reached the peak and from that vantage point
Could see no end
While in the dark hours now
I see the blue horizon endless
And the moonlit castle high upon the crag
That took our breath away one breathless day
Never did the sea look more
Serene to me, inviting me to sleep
And dream of skylarks singing as the noontide flows
around us locked together on the shore

Cynthia Watson, Knaresborough, North Yorkshire

FISHERMAN

His face is tanned to living leather,
the lines on his brow
measure winter storms and poor catches.

HIs voice recalls the sea,
low, like booming rollers
and wrapped up in a deep blue gansey.

His smile promises
days of calm waters,
light breezes and fish.

He stands proud, surveying his world,
thirty-four feet long, by a lifetime wide
and he wouldn't change an inch.

Brian Morton, Redcar, North Yorkshire

REVELATION

Their heads are close.
Downy curls brush thin grey strands. I sidle round them.
Knowing palms cradle tiny fingers
as each bulb is carried to the bowl.
Together they sprinkle on more soil and press it firm.
The bulbs are hidden.
Granny says they will come to life again.
The child tries to grasp flakes of fallen skin.
Her elfin breath wafts them over the table's edge.
I lift my daughter to the sink.
She stretches out her hands, showing dark sickles under
the nails.

Black shod, we pick our way between the stones.
The polished oak is lowered.
Coarse straps scrape against the planed joints. It is hard to
believe where she is. The thud of soil is absorbed.
I can see nothing.
Drawing a hand across my face, I examine
a dark stain on the leather. My left arm hangs limp.
Determined fingers seek out mine.
No need to look.

Kat Dale, York, North Yorkshire

THE ENTERTAINER

He was playing a Joplin rag.
Repeating the first bars,
as if he couldn't move on;
as if he didn't want us to move on.

Back home with the sheets
he could take us A to Z.
A history of the bordello
on the upright, small hours
reeling under forty watts.

Out there, memory shrugging by the
far wall, he went with what he knew;
kept on playing what he knew.

Deep inside, he is playing still.
No more, and never less than I remember,
and at the table of ghosts we listen.
Measuring life. Marking time.

Tony Noon, Mexborough, South Yorkshire

PERFECT TIMING

In our former lives, it was you
who turned me upside down
as I somersaulted athletically
to meet your every need,
until the demand for soft boiled eggs
I thought I detected a pattern;
having once lived with a man
who took a hard line on burnt toast;
recalling my father's intolerance of over-cooked peas.
It seemed our love would be strangled
on the yoke of your unmet desire.
Your untimely death provided the answer:
Now I have your ashes in an egg-timer;
Daily I turn you upside down
as deliverance percolates through
your precisely measured remains.

Mary Louise Carr, Sheffield, South Yorkshire

STARFISH STRANDED

The sun has not yet spoken to the day
And I wander the wave-washed shingle
Looking for the footprints of the night
Long lost to the anger of the tides
Moonfaced innocence that lit your smile.

This place which holds yesteryear
Hidden in Eros' eroding clay,
Speaks of rituals that walked these
Shingled shores before my awakening
To the lunar love's spectacle of spirits.

In the sun-warming salty waters
I find reflecting from the rocks
Dark glare, a stranded starfish gifted
To the day by the magic of the night
And the music of the waves.

Lifting the star from the crystal pool
For in the dream I watched it die
As did that love unknown to you or I,
Then in silent prayer I made a wish
And returned it to the evening sky.

Keith Garrett, Wath-upon-Dearne, Rotherham, South
Yorkshire

THE WRECK

You caught me,
Basking in the sun -
Aeons of rest
On this bed of time.
Good English oak
Rough-gnawed by the tides -
I stink of weed
And sea-soaked wood.

Yet must you touch
My bleached white bones;
Tickle my back
With bare brown feet,
As the sand silts up
My rotting teeth,
And the shells crack sharp
In my splintered skin.

Jean Armitage, Liversedge, West Yorkshire

THE PAINTER

He goes home alone and paints with his mind,
Re-creating in thought, not with brush, the red-pink,
Deep grey-purple of sunset. No sun, just the light it reflects
Caught up in the clouds. He swills wine or tea around his
mouth,
Splashing the sides of a dark unseen easel; a flexing tongue
Is the artist's palate, tasting and mixing the colours. Soon,
maybe
Next time, he'll lift that sky bruised by beauty and take it
with him.

Nebulous forms elongated, stretches of cloud as if a blot of
paint
Had beens smudged unthinkingly by some giant index
finger. More
Glimpses of eternal sun, he must imprint the full true
colour on
His mind - where it will stay and never reach canvas. Home
Alone, he draws upon memories mixed up, folded in on one
another -
Which colour? Which shape? He takes all colours and
blends
Thickly, smoothly but with rough hands. "There," he says
as
The wall drips chaos.

Julie-Ann Maude, Morley, West Yorkshire

CANOEING AT EAST MARTON

Light-hearted we slide out of the sun
And paddle under arching trees.
Water pleats under the prow,
But beside us, still as glass,
Our reflecting faces
Moon in a wreath of leaves.

Two centuries ago,
Where our ghost heads swim,
The navvies shovelled,
Breath darting needles in thin chests.

Driven sheep puddled
With tiny stamping feet
The gouged-out clay
Until at last the water rose.
The groans and bleating stilled
And trees grew silently.

We dip our paddles, leave a bubbled scar,
And, deep in thought,
Glide swiftly from the dark,
Into the bright, limed light.

Barbara Roberts, Wetherby, West Yorkshire

TOUCH AND TURN

my fingers touch the drawer to open
delicately place the disc
close again and press the play sign
set the level, lose the hiss

her voice, it touches ears and opens
softly places sounds in air
closes off my other senses
levels out in some lost layer

something spinning at the centre
something turning in the heart
seam of sadness, called to motion
mined and melted by her art

Andy Vowles, Leeds, West Yorkshire

Wales

UNSPOKEN

As the rain beats on its window drum,
On a rainy night in March
I'll assign myself the task in hand,
Of deciphering your thoughts.
Body language,
Motions,
A language in itself,
Stealing glances here and there,
Eyes meet
Then they melt.
Supercharging silence,
Atmosphere weighed down,
Tension you could chew on,
Your coyness is your crown.

Matt Lightfoot, Wrexham, Wales

DEATH OF A SOLDIER

He stood by here
Heard the waves
Smother the rocks
Drag the shingle

Heard the lone curlew
Call at ebb tide
Over Welsh sand.
Smelled the sea

Used them for a well
In a hot place and dry
Carried our burden.
No more than a boy

James McKeon, Newport, Wales

I CAME I WENT

Lost in the desert of life's desires
Seared by the heat in timeless sand,
Buried deep in memories,
each sifted through the glass of hours,
Where grain by grain each second speaks its
own beginning,
Then spills its end upon the palm of
nature's hand.
What secrets lie entombed above, below?
Untouched by the fates of countless years,
Like footprints forever lost upon the tide,
As if marooned upon a lake of glass,
Briefly mirrored, and like all ephemeral things
Just mere reflections,
As with all shadows lost in the darkness,
Gone, no more espied.
No trace remains of thee or me,
All that we were like all desires lie spent,
We depart not really knowing
Why we came or went.

Gary Price, Powys, Wales

THE GOLDEN ROAD - MYNYDD PRESELI

The basalt outcrops echo to the raven's guttural croak
And sky is filled with warbled song
As lark, unseen assures his mate
That all is well.

Trivial sounds, a distant bleat, a chirp
A gentle breeze, a buzzing bee
Mayflies meet, caress, converse, disperse
And dance for pleasure of themselves and me.

In sphagnum lies the purest water
I have ever seen.
I drink as they before me drank
Whoever put it there I thank.

Before I was and others listened
As this way they came
They left their mark, but now have gone
And I must do the same.

So when I've gone and others come
To listen to the lark
Perhaps they'll read this epitaph
For it will be my mark.

Philip Poole, Pembroke Dock, Wales

DECEMBER

Dark winter presses against the window,
earth sodden after eighty days of rain.
They long for light, the brightness of snow.

Another day of grey rain and cloud so low.
These short December days are all the same
with dark winter pressed against the window.

The floods have taken over the meadow,
turned grass to mud, no time to drain.
They long for light, the brightness of snow.

They wanted crisp days, brisk winds to blow
to dry up the water on sodden plains,
but dark winter pressed against the window.

The descent to solstice without the glow
of crisp mornings, the sparkle of frost again.
They long for light, the brightness of snow.

Storms and flooded rivers. They need to know
that this wet weather will not remain
while dark winter presses against the window.
They long for light, the brightness of snow.

Sue Moules, Lampeter, Wales

SEPTUAGENARIAN HUES

Thirty thousand sun-engineered dawns
Have vanished, since sunlight first puckered a baby's face
Feeding from a timorous teenage mum.
Infant eyes then open in wonder of curvilinear fantasies
Triggered by a twig tip, made incandescent through trial by
fire,
Contriving retained images of ellipses and figures of eight.
Pure mathematics distancing to matriculation.
Your country needs you, youth! Days of stress and woe,
When Britain alone confronts the foe.
Young men in the navy, airforce blue. Hurrah for the
Hussars.
The spirit of Britain, driving away the beast to his den,
Illuminating the way of truth again.
Then the embryonic oneness, to develop and envelop,
A love transcending treasures of silver, pearl, ruby and
olympian gold
Appealing grand and great descendants,
Ah, yesterday, yesteryear!
Static pictures, held in mind's frame -
Dynamic when bathed in the bathos of time.
Look back in gratitude, old man, look back to live.
Nil desperandum - the best is yet to come.

Alun Bannister, Bishopston, Wales

LIFE WILL FORGIVE

Bitter thoughts wash away as dawn unfolds
the coming day
Old man's memories, young man's dreams
as winter snow becomes mountain streams
Bygone days reminisce, sweethearts smile
lovers kiss
Conquests remembered rejections forgotten
streets of life unwind as a reel of cotton
Nurture your dreams, fulfil your desires
life will forgive if at least you aspire

David Coleman, Mold, Wales

CONFRONTATION

"I'm pregnant, and I'm on the streets."
Confusion makes me pause
How should I act? Avert my gaze?
Side-step, pretend I haven't heard,
Ashamed of having been approached,
Contaminated by this seamy side of life?
I struggle to assert respectability,
To hang on to the "norm" conform
I dare not lose my place - communicate
Believe in her reality
It's all a con - she's trying to take me for a ride
They're all the same, they've got it made.
The cliches crowd!
And thus I cannot give the coin,
That would admit
That she is pregnant on the streets,
For then, like Christ, I must give all.

Joan Conway, Holywell, Wales

REVELATION

Gliding down Paradise Road
Arms entwined and hearts in time
Fluid hips reaching and stepping
Blessed with shared virtuostic cadence.

Sideways glance
Dopamine kicks, the adrenaline rush
A fourth dimension of transparent pleasure,
deep kissed
Shibboleths and sacred cows scattered and shattered
Their sacred sacrament, simple truth
Unzipped, stripped bare of frippery
Proud for all to see, released from the flotsam of crushing
mediocrity
Giving velour-coated tenderness.

Faces lashed and passed by horizontal hail
Lifted from the surf's spray
Laced with the essence of crafted pine
Dashing hurriedly on in the search of Gladstone's chiselled
memory

They turn for home in ice dance symmetry
Light of step, high of spirit
Sharing the ambrosia of Venus.

Philip Davies, Conwy, Wales

SONNET TO HAND-ROLLED GOLDEN VIRGINIA

You are right. It does come first. White
touchpaper thin as a host, then gunpowder,
fuse, and the rest will follow, sure as breath.
Little promethean acts that set the word
alight. Ritual origami for the spiritually lost.
Forgive the quick intimacy at bars and parties,
for we know each other in the lung, the heart;
smoke-screen wizards all. And I, a good enough
person otherwise. I take the stairs. Buy vegetables.
Am a paid-up member of Amnesty International.
I hold down a job, between fag-breaks. Angel I am
not. Everyone needs forgiving. So forgive me, but
I won't quit. And if this helps you to overlook my
other, many, far more grave shortcomings, so be it.

Tiffany Atkinson, Aberystwyth, Wales

THE COVER

Lying crumpled shining
abandoned on the desk.
Your colour tempts,
your inside beckons.
Once opened and popped
your centre revealed.
The sweetness melts inside
and then you are discarded,
rolled into a ball, your colour wrapped with
shining
and all that's left is the fragrant aroma and the prize is
gone.
You are cast off into the bin
Sweet wrapper, I'll miss you.

John Latus, Johnstown, Carmarthen, Wales

YORE

I am standing on Heather Mountain
Looking for the gems, I threw away long ago
In the white remembered days of my youth
Days of marsh marigold remembrance
Of swallow-owned evenings yore
Of willow green, arches high
Bird song downpour in leafy lanes
With tinkling water in mountain brook brown

Away to the sea, of school age youngness yore
Firstly on a sailing ketch billowing white
Later on cargo ships, blue funnel's finest
All named from Greek mythology
Elpenor, Cyclops and many other steam leviathans
Deep sea east to Penang, sunrise sunset azores west
Later home to my Heather Mountain, drizzle hued

Wyn Williams, Caernarfon, Wales

THE SEA

I could not dwell but by the sea
The sound alone breathes life on me
Waves that crash on rocky strand
Or gently lap on golden sand,
The oyster catcher's friendly trill,
The black gulls scream through open bill,
The salty spray my life revives.
Like the changing colour of the skies
To watch its everchanging face,
Dark and angry but with wild grace.
Then tumbled gaily on the shore
With merry tune, not mighty roar,
I would not live save by the brine,
There nature sparkles like good wine,
To wander on the high tide mark,
And gather shells or tooth of shark
Or stand upon a sand dune high,
And dream of those good days gone by,
Drake, Raleigh, Nelson brave and free,
Who loved the sea as much as me.

B G Metcalfe, Porthcawl, Wales

WRECKAGES

In the rank hollow of that stream
(clogged with putrescent car cases
of thieved and dumped Fiestas and Novas),
shaken by the memory of joy, I prayed.

Thick, mephitic mud sticking to the sole,
I grasped a slimed-over branch
that dripped discoloured rain onto the slope;
above me, a goldfinch host of high vermillion.

Wheels of cloud lay wrecked on bars of light,
while the wind-fingered wreckages,
bogged into landscape, sang like a rogue
Aeolian harp. It raised the nap

of my skin. I walk the dog again tomorrow,
across the ridge and down to the stream,
singing to myself, but unable to carry a tune,
my ears caught between goldfinch

and steelwreck.

Kevin Mills, Hengoed, Wales

REFLECTING SYMMETRY

What does it reflect,
the bedroom mirror?
- Symmetrical moons
of your breasts,
perfect cleft
of your buttocks,
and as you undress -
each curved thigh
soft mirror to each other,
convexities,
concavities of flesh
leave me spellbound.

Sometimes your striptease
teases me;
tonight, fatigued,
I bury my face in my pillow -
symmetrically we sink into sleep,
and the body of the bed,
swallows us,
whole.

Marc Harris, Cardiff, Wales

Northern Ireland

SAILS

"Have you got dreams?" The old man said.
"Oh yes!" Said the little boy.
"My dreams are sails to ride on
Like clouds in a wind-blown sky.
My dreams are my strength and fortitude,
When hopes just pass me by."

The old man turned
And stumbled
On the tear that filled his eye.

Joseph Hughes, Newtownards, Northern Ireland

NO COMFORT

No comfort can the poet feel
when images
he thought sublime
cannot find a resting place
in hearts and minds of lesser kind.

The soul may bleed
upon the page
leave hieroglyphs to point the way
but mortals tire of constant search
for meaning in the metaphor.

The nectared tones the gods
will savour
too rich by far for common man
like caviar with salty flavour
make him yearn for cakes and ale.

Denis O'Sullivan, Newtownabbey, Northern Ireland

TEMPTATION

If we could have seen that fatal fruit,
Had we been there at dawn of time,
Would we too have unleashed this demon,
Ate of the fruit that was solely forbidden?

There it hung from slender tree:
Scarlet satin enclosing sacred white flesh.

Reach out and touch its untouched skin.
Could something so sweet be such a sin?

Reach out and pluck it from the tree.
It wants to be tasted; it needs to be set free.

Bite deep.
Juice pours from your mouth.
Soft, succulent flesh of the seducer -
Savour.
You have eaten.

The seeds of this fruit,
Inherent in your genes.

Christa Brodie, Ballymena, Northern Ireland

ALL MEMORIES ARE OF YOU NOW

When I was a boy I watched
the sunset reflect in an iron pool
but the bronze beams and the royal blue skies
are all gone now.
Their colour stolen for your hair
and your eyes.

I long for you in the pit of midnight
and I chew the bitter black petals
of words that should have been spoken
It is a giant's love I hold for you
in this little man's heart.

Tony Weir, Belfast, Northern Ireland

ROOM WITH A VIEW

Glance out the window for just one moment.
Pause ...
Inhale it, recording each detail in your mind.

Notice the birds, their beauty in flight,
The hills that surround
As the sky turns to night.
Taste it, feel it.
Steal the scene: A lifetime of creation,
A painter's dream.

Ponder your existence,
The nature of your life,
Surrender to the placid, tranquil side of life.
Own it, define it,
This is your life:
Don't let this moment pass you by,
Just glance outside ...

Lisa Warr, Lisburn, Northern Ireland

THE BALLAD OF THE COCONUT KISSES

Honey, I've never
Said anything kind
And soft to you -
Oh so sweet words
To buy you a song.
I tear at you constantly
With jagged baby teeth,
The pollution I spread
Hangs grey and heavy -
Elephants plodding.

Under the simple sky
I wish to sprinkle you with sugar
To lie with you,
Wafting coconut kisses
Along the puzzle of your spine
Forever entwined,
Indefatigable.

Rowena Foster, Portadown, Northern Ireland

Scotland

IN EARLY AUTUMN

In our lakeside woodland I looked
for bright leaves to press.
Yellowing elms, claret cherries
sunburnt beeches,
chestnut speckle all colours
birches make ochre snow
And oaks empty from their trees like brown
jigsaw pieces

At the pathside, low down
I came upon an umbrella mosaic,
a bramble bristling with sharpened spikes,
the kind that get under you nails,
sting with purple spite,
offer only hard berries, and flies

I lifted the leaves on suspicion
and underneath lay a dipping cluster
of swollen to bursting berries untouched
Black purple, purple black, full of juice

It was worth the stained fingers
the tiny thorns, to swallow those berries
remembering the blaze of childhood

Vivien Jones, Powfoot, Annan, Scotland

NO MAP FOR LOVE

We make little journeys
into each others uncertainty
Travelling without
the map for love
Lying in wait of destiny

This is a wondrous voyage
Let no pirate raise
the skull and crossbones here
Let no frown
or fallen tear appear
Should we slip away from laughter
Let us wait for some blonde
and solid shore

John McLeod, Thurso, Scotland

IN THE DEAD OF THE NIGHT

Under the pergola we slipped into bliss,
Intoxicated with the moonlit night;
Blessed to witness on such a night as this
The garden awash with infinite light.
The oak-leafed hydrangea, each bloom a cloud,
Luminesces in the dark of the bower;
The weeping birch droops, its branches a shroud,
To the lily beneath, in late flower.
The wooden bench warm from hours of sun,
The snap of a leaf as it falls onto the stone,
Our hands intertwined, the day almost done,
We sit on transfixed, together, alone.
In the dead of the night we awaken,
In this peace and this stillness born again.

Patricia Ace, Crieff, Scotland

MOTHER OF THE BRIDE

Her kisses were too lush
too greedy,
lips damp as limpets
fastening on rock.

In that great cavern of a hall
her pink hat eddied through the crowd
a blossom tossed upon the tide.
Her arms were sea-anemonies
hungry to embrace.

Refugees from bonhomie
sheltered in the bar,
were we wrong to be
both judge and jury?

But her kisses were too lush
too greedy.
She fed upon her guests.
It was unseemly
to make a feast of courtesy
to kiss and smile and kiss and kiss
as though it were her day.

Catherine Orr, Barrhead, Scotland

FORBIDDING MOURNING

The dead,
Gathering round their own
Funeral pyres,
Hollow-eyed, mute witnesses
To empty elegies and
Fraudulent laments,
Wail.

What are these unnatural goodbyes
But a way for the living
To purge their guilt.

No roses,
Blood red, milk white
For me. No
Sham speeches
From mock preachers.
Bury me standing up,
With a sword.

Andrew Kerr, Auldgirth, Dumfries, Scotland

SYMBIOSIS

It's like this -

he makes her presents:

a set of photographs
from their first developed film,
glued together and tied with string;

a recycled jar of blank confetti,
the shapes from poems
he'll never write;

and on Valentine's Day a single
transparency with a heart cut out -
he keeps the heart out of sight.

Perhaps he gives her all
she wants, and he has all he needs;
she holds for him a prism -

he catches rainbow light.

Jennifer Elliott, Balmullo, Scotland

WIPERS

Mundane existing, broken,
by the wiper's rhythmic
funnelling of raindrops,
into rippling streams
of thoughts.
Transfixed I watch
my concentration
roll down the windows ...
Flooded in soothing numbness,
I drift.

R M Membury, Culloden, Scotland

CUPPED HANDS

There is certainty about love.

Like water in cupped hands
It will seep through,
Fall to earth,
And find its way back to the ocean.

Not long ago,
Fearing I would find no more,
I squeezed my hands tight,
Desperately holding
To that which I had.

Now,
With arms open wide,
I stand in a downpour.

Graham Brown, Darnaway, Scotland

FLOTSAM

Inside a dragon carved chest
which still smells of camphor
trophies from the coral reef.
I wore dainty rubber slippers -
protected against the stone fish
I dived deeper than anyone
and never felt the spikes.
Dried seaweed clings to a conch
all the noise has gone.

Maureen Macnaughtan, Glenrothes, Scotland

TIMELESS

The same old tune
Crackling in its dotage,
Unsure as a faint
Childhood memory

Still they play it.

Loyally dropping a penny in the slot,
A satisfying clink.
Pushing the button,
Faint and smudged with use.
The speakers crackle into life
Sounding a piece known by
Rusty, mechanical heart,
As they sit back,
Sinking into silent nostalgia.

Jennifer Speirs, Thornhill, Stirling, Scotland

WHERE DO THE FLAMES GO?

Where do the flames go
When candles expire?
Where bides the comfort
When dull dies the fire?

Where rests the echo
When spent is the shout?
Where stands steady faith
When vanquished by doubt?

Where goes the laughter
At end of the play?
Where rests the sunbeam
At the end of the day?

Where sleep the dreams
When dreamers awake?
Where fly the vows
When lovers forsake?

Where melts the rainbow
When rain and sun part?
When will the pain go
You left in my heart?

Colin Dennison, Stranraer, Scotland

IN THE GLASS HOUSE

This house of love and endless light
We populate, and know no sin,
With sunny hearts and souls, pure white
Until the toil and grief seep in.
All doors are locked, but nothing riles
With doubt or curiosity
The lifeless eyes and ersatz smiles
That cut each new atrocity.
Our palace of transparent walls
With windows wrought with boundless views
Detaches us when darkness falls,
And guests arrive with pleasant news
For we won't leave this house, house of cards
These polished panes; our labour's lumber;
There's nothing left, save broken shards,
The broken mirror, shards of lifelong slumber.
And yet we prize the lapsing years
While every backward step we take
Trails frozen fears, and diamond tears
Of sorrow in our dormant wake.

Matthew Smith-Mearns, Aberdeen, Scotland

A LETTER I NEVER SENT YOU

Picasso's caressing a Monet,

Pointillist poetry dripping its blood
On a cold, cold canvas,
His eyes brimful with
Triangular tears,
Guernica slipping a comforting arm
Around his heaving shoulders,

And not a soul to understand
Why he should weep.

Alan Carter, Rothesay, Isle of Bute, Scotland

WALNEY WINTER

The wintry shore
Rocks hunched against the wind
The sand shivers.

Birds cry
For summers past
Gathering flocks
Departing.

The silver sea
Low winter sun
Grey blanket skies
Unfolding.

Running footsteps
Children's cries
Echoes of warmer days
And sea-washed castles.

Anne Dunford, Newton Stewart, Scotland

DESPONDENT OF SLOUGH

As I lie, I hear the drunks go by
Shouting, fighting, swearing, being sick.
Mature products of mature democracy
Advanced civilisation at its apogee.

My neighbour beats his wife, I see
Her bruises, feel her pain see no gain
Maturely in a mature democracy
Advancing civilizedly.

My job pays six pounds an hour
Servicing people just like you
Profiting from mature capital democracy
Advanced interest civilisation.

History is clear on this, unequivocal
Decadence brings destruction in its wake
Come gentle bombs and fall on ... you
There's not much left of civilization now.

Steven Hepburn, Edinburgh, Scotland

NARCISSUS

Winter morning bus
In the warm chatter, chatter
Dozing in and out of reality.
My face in the navy blue window.
A bit Greta-Garbo-ish wouldn't you say?
Pity about the raindrop acne!
Hurtling towards daybreak I grow insubstantial.

Marta Blackadder, Tobermory, Isle of Mull, Scotland

CONVERSATION WITH POSEIDON

Seeking to show Earth's treasure to another
I have flung to the waves
What I loved on land.
This I done I found
all transformed in the image of the sea.
The scarab beetle became a crab,
the winter blackbird turned to coalfish,
fields of hay were sea grass
and the rice grains, pearls.
Finally I flung to the waves the sun and moon
but they too drowned in those fertile depths,
becoming a tapestry
of watered light.

Colin Dewar, Dumfries, Scotland

BLACKCURRANTS

She sat cross-legged
in sprigged pyjamas
brown eyes testimony
to a treacle-black history
sticky with guilt.

Breakfast was late
that May day
hot with sun-washed
forgiveness and hope.

Soft and pliable
slabs of white bread
on tangerine plates
oozing blackcurrants
on her brand new day.

A blackcurrant jam day
tasting of tomorrow
sweet with charity
and full-bellied faith.

Louise Laurie, Ayr, Scotland

LANCELOT

He loves her
as mortal man loves.

Sees her flaws
yet knows
his own
as far from slight
so loves her
those despite.

But that is not
what she wants.

She wants
love like wolves.
Like flame.

Fierce. Brilliant.
Ultimately
doomed.

She wants perfection.
She wants Lancelot.

Lesley-Anne Reid, Dundee, Scotland